SOMETHING'S COMING . . . SOMETHING GREAT

Sermons For Advent,
Christmas And Epiphany
Cycle A First Lesson Texts

BY ROBERT A. BERINGER

C.S.S. Publishing Co., Inc.
Lima, Ohio

SOMETHING'S COMING . . . SOMETHING GREAT

Library of Congress Cataloging-in-Publication Data

Beringer, Robert, 1936-
    Something's coming — something great : sermons for Advent, Christmas and Epiphany : cycle A first lesson texts / by Robert A. Beringer.
    p.   c.m
    ISBN 1-55673-428-X
    1. Advent sermons. 2. Christmas sermons. 3. Epiphany season — sermons.
4. Bible. O.T. — Sermons. 5. Sermons, American. I. Title.
BV4254.5.B475   1992
252'.61—dc20
    92-4583
    CIP

9231 / ISBN 1-55673-428-X

PRINTED IN U.S.A.

In Gratitude To

Peggy, David, Peter, Beth, and Tom

And for all they have taught
me about the wonder of God's amazing love.

Table Of Contents

Introduction

Finding ways to help the message of the Advent — Christmas season come alive is always a challenge for most pastors. I am grateful to the editors at C.S.S. for this opportunity to rediscover the excitement and anticipation of the Old Testament writers as they stood on tiptoe, waiting for God to act on the stage of human history.

I have chosen as a title for this collection of sermons the words from one of the songs in Leonard Bernstein's popular musical, *West Side Story*. The song, "Something's Coming," catches the spirit of the Advent season, and the hope that sustained the Hebrew people through the period of their captivity and despair.

Although each of these chapters is based on an Old Testament text, I have tried to make these messages Christ-centered in every way. My prayer is that you, the reader, will find a blessing in these words, and that you will be both challenged and comforted as together we consider the wonder of the Word become flesh in Jesus Christ our Lord.

Robert A. Beringer

Advent 1
Isaiah 2:1-5

"Something's Coming"

Could it be? Who knows?
There's something to anything,
  I will know right away, soon as it shows.
It may come cannonballing down from the sky —
Who knows?

It's just out of reach . . . down the block . . .
  on a beach . . . under a tree,
I got a feeling there's a miracle goin' to
  come true, coming to me!

Could it be? Yes, it could . . . Something's comin',
  something good if I can wait.
Something's comin', I don't know what it is,
  but it's going to be great!
Something's comin' — don't go away![1]

Perhaps you recognize those words from the opening song of Leonard Bernstein's hit Broadway musical, *West Side Story*. "Something's comin' . . . something great!" — those words catch the spirit of the first Sunday of the Advent season and Isaiah's great vision of peace over all the earth. For Isaiah believed with all his heart that God would one day bring about a world where all humankind would live together and walk together before the Lord in faith, righteousness and peace.

Let's not miss the power that such a great vision has given to God's people in every age. Isaiah wrote these words when his own people were weary of the bloody wars with Syria, and it looked as if the nation was condemned to one awful war after another until the whole human family destroyed itself.

God's people in another age took heart from these same words and others like them that promised a kingdom of God on this earth — a time when God's rule over all the earth would be supreme, when Christ would return in power and glory. That vision was all that kept those early Christians going in the face of bloody persecution and hardship. Like Isaiah of old they stood on tiptoe, believing that God would cause something great, something fabulous, to happen on this earth. Words almost failed the writers of the Bible as they looked forward to God's great future. Isaiah pictured the Lord's house set up on a high mountain with the nations of the world streaming toward that mountain, swords beaten into plowshares and spears beaten into pruning hooks. God's people in every age have strained their eyes towards the horizons of history — something is about to happen!

Now, while skeptics will laugh at such dreams and hopes, we all know how looking forward to some great event adds a zest and hope and expectancy to our everyday lives. Expectant parents find real joy in assembling a new crib, or painting the nursery, or practicing all that pushing and breathing. Residents of a town excitedly begin mowing lawns, sweeping sidewalks, repairing the windows on the town hall and hanging bunting on all the buildings when some dignitary or celebrity is coming to town.

Even the coming of Christmas has this kind of power to send people into action. The world may not even know what Advent is or when it begins, but for months now everyone has known that Christmas is coming. A high school teacher was in the barber shop last year just before Christmas. He and the barber were talking about how much the kids look forward to their Christmas vacation.

"Yes," said the teacher, "you should have seen the excitement on the last day of school. There was foot-stomping, back-slapping, table-pounding, singing and shouts of joy — and all that was only in the teachers' lounge!"

Yes, we all know the excitement that a future possibility can bring to our daily lives. But if we are honest about it, we have also experienced the sense of loss and disappointment over a hoped for future that does not come. Is there anyone who has not known the emptiness, the despair, the heartache, when, in spite of all our preparations, nothing really happens? The young wife and husband try with frantic desperation to conceive a child, but it seems to be all in vain. The town prepares for the celebrity's visit, but the parade is canceled because the dignitary made a last-minute change in route and bypassed the town! For many people, even Christmas Day brings a deep disappointment. The beautiful packages are opened, gifts are admired and then put away. Trees come down. Shepherds and angels are stored away in boxes for another year. The long-awaited day seems to pass with a sense that nothing — nothing — has really happened.

In a far more profound way, God's people have always had to live with their eyes on a distant future. For people in Isaiah's time, the vision of a coming Messiah sounded wonderful. But the only ones who came were the Assyrians and the Persians with their conquering armies. The early Christians prayed fervently for their Lord's return, "Come, Lord Jesus." But it was Roman soldiers who came, not the Christ of God in power and glory. And many people in today's world will dismiss this vision of God's wondrous future as simply the talk of foolish dreamers. Where is that day when, as Paul puts it, "every knee shall bow and every tongue confess that Jesus Christ is Lord?" Where is this wonderful God-shaped future when we seem to be sinking in oceans of human need and hunger and poverty? Where is this God-shaped future when human greed is like a bottomless pit? Where is the time in our strife-torn world when spears will become pruning hooks and swords will be changed into plowshares?

We try bravely to make light of the despair and hopelessness in our world. A recent cartoon shows an old man watching the morning news on television. The announcer says, "A Poland Spring tanker truck carrying 50,000 gallons of fresh water crashed into a Pawtucket Exxon gas station this morning, causing massive contamination of the super unleaded tanks." Yes, we try to make light of the world's greed and godlessness, but is something ever going to happen? Is this vision of a kingdom of God on earth just another pious fantasy? If it is, then the Church of Jesus Christ is just another well-meaning institution in our society whistling its hymns in the dark, collecting the pledge cards, passing the offering plates, and keeping the mimeograph humming. In reality, it is like the rest of the world, expecting nothing to really happen — nothing to change!

But Isaiah was no dreamer! People of faith in every age have found hope in this great dream of a Sovereign God ruling over this world in a way that once and for all will bring an end to the war and the fear that grips our hearts. Isaiah's vision is based on two great realities that we must not only remember but we must also celebrate afresh on the first Sunday of Advent.

1. In God's Own Good Time

Isaiah reminds us first that the promised kingdom of God will come in all its fullness in God's own good time. He writes, "In days to come, the mountain of the Lord's house shall be established . . . ." His words are echoed in the New Testament by Jesus who when speaking of the coming of God's Messiah a second time into our world said, "Of that day or that hour no one knows, not even the angels of heaven, nor the Son, but only the Father." Bluntly put, the writers of the Bible say that God's future will not arrive when we want it, plan it, or even when we think we need it. It will not come on Hal Lindsay's timetable (author of *The Late Great Planet Earth*) nor even on the timetable of the President of the United States! It will come in God's own good time because our God is not in the business of providing happy endings for the futures we are engineering! What Isaiah saw and Jesus foretold is a future so magnificent and so far beyond our knowledge and control that not even the angels of heaven know when it is coming. You see, Isaiah's vision is based on the faith that this world will never know peace and harmony and goodwill until all human beings acknowledge God as their Sovereign Lord. Leaving God out of our lives gives us the kind of world we know today. But, putting God at the center of our thinking and planning and living, we can even now begin to catch a foretaste of the great and wondrous time when Christ will be Lord of all. That foretaste is really what we celebrate on this first Sunday in Advent. For when God's own Son went obediently to the cross to die for the sins of the world, and was then raised from the dead in glorious resurrection power, the world got a glimpse of God's final assault on the powers of evil and sin. In that now familiar comparison, Christ's death and resurrection were God's D-Day, reminiscent of the Allied Forces landing on the Normandy beaches in the Second World War. Those forces had many battles left to fight, but D-Day marked the beginning of the end of the Nazi forces and VE-Day was assured. God's Victory Day is coming, but it will come in God's own good time because it is the Sovereign God who rules this world, not us.

2. Today In The Light Of Tomorrow

But Isaiah's words remind us of something else to be remembered and celebrated on this first Sunday of the Advent Season. God is calling us to live today in the light of God's tomorrow. Disasters, both national and personal, are part and parcel of life in this world. We cannot always tell what part bereavement, loss, illness and defeat play in the great plan of God nor would the realities of those experiences be lessened for us if we knew the whole plan. Instead, the Christian must always look beyond the present to the future; it is there that the explanation ultimately lies. The world around us wants to use the scientific principle of cause and effect to explain human history; in other words, it is yesterday that explains today. But in the Christian experience, it may well be tomorrow that best explains today. As my former teacher, John Hick, has written, "If there is any eventual resolution of the interplay between good and evil, any decisive bringing of good out of evil, it must lie beyond this world and beyond the enigma of death." For the Christian, certainly, "the best is yet to be."

That means that every moment of the passing day is already alive with the promise of God's future bearing upon us. Like Isaiah of old, those who trust in the promise of God's coming kingdom know that history must have an ending, and that God must be a part of that ending! Those who trust in the promise of God's coming kingdom are able to see the advance signs that, even now, something is about to happen.

Every time we as a congregation recite those time-honored words from the Apostles' Creed, "He will come to judge the quick and the dead . . . ," we are disclosing our hope that there will be a day when God's justice will be greater than anything we see today in a world dominated by good lawyers and fat checkbooks. Every time a congregation like ours creates a food pantry or a clothing bank, we do so, not in the naive hope that a few cans of soup and an old suit will solve all human need, but in the light of that great banquet table in heaven where no one will hunger and all will gather in peace and love. Every time a Christian speaks a word of forgiveness in a situation of bitterness and hatred, that Christian is speaking in the future present tense. We are giving the world a foretaste of how God will help us to live together in God's kingdom. Come, let us walk in the light of the Lord! Every time a congregation stands up and sings from the heart, "Come, Thou Long-Expected Jesus, Born To Set Thy People Free," we are joining Isaiah in the prayer that one day that whole world will indeed walk in the light of the Lord. Every time we sing those words, we are celebrating our conviction that someone is coming, someone great! Even so, Come Lord Jesus!

God's Christmas Greeting

Christmas is the time of year for sending messages. That's why the postal service estimates some five billion Christmas cards and letters will be mailed in the next few weeks. By anyone's standard, that's a lot of money, time and trouble invested in sending a message of good news to friends and family.

But messages are important, and for many of us, Christmas is the only time in the year when we hear from old and distant friends. Christmas is a time when God sends a message to the world as well, and these words from Isaiah bring us a message from the Lord that we long to hear. This ancient prophet was called upon to be God's message-bearer to a people who had lived in despair and misery as captives of the Babylonians. The Hebrews were a despised people, displaced persons who lived in a world that had been turned upside down. Their daily lives were filled with injustice and conflict, and there was little in which they could take courage. But Isaiah was chosen of God to bring a message of good news, and the prophet's beautiful vision may well be the same kind of message God wishes to send us in this Advent Season.

1. Hope In The Midst Of Despair

Isaiah's first words are words of hope in the midst of despairing times: "There shall come forth a shoot from the

15

stump of Jesse . . . ." Now this is much more than some twig that begins to grow out of a dead stump. The Hebrew words suggest a strong healthy branch, tough new growth on a tree that has long produced much good fruit. In this case the new branch is a king from the house of David whose gifts come directly from God and under whose leadership, all life will be changed. Now this hope is good news for the poor, the meek and the oppressed, and bad news for the unrighteous, the sinful and the oppressors. It reminds me a little of those good news-bad news stories that were so popular a few years ago. I still chuckle over the old golfer who could not imagine what life would be like without his daily round. One day he consulted a spiritualist, asking her if she thought there would be golf courses in heaven. She meditated for a few moments and then said to the old golfer, "I have some good news and some bad news for you. The good news is that heaven is filled with lush, green golf courses with lavish club houses. The bad news is that you are scheduled to tee off on one of those heavenly golf courses tomorrow morning at 9:30!"

Good news and bad news — the hope that God promises in the midst of despair is a message that forces us to see our world for what it has become in its brokenness and sinfulness. To be sure Christmas is coming, but in Central America the destroying, the killing and the oppression are daily facts of life. Christmas is coming, but the very fabric of our society is threatened by new realities called drug wars, drug lords and drug traffic. Christmas is coming but for those who live in the Middle East, all talk of peace and good will seems to be little more than empty rhetoric. Christmas is coming but the FBI says that every 54 seconds a violent crime occurs in this nation, a robbery every other minute, and another woman violated by rape every 17 minutes.

Let's not pretty up God's Christmas greeting so much that we miss the real reason why Christ came into our broken world. Christ came as the fulfillment of Isaiah's vision of a whole new order. Christ came to change both the hearts of humankind and the society in which we live. Christ came to call

16

us to repentance and to turn us away from all the lesser gods who have usurped the place of the Living God on the throne of our hearts. That's the real hope that God has always offered to a world in the midst of despair. It's a hope that calls us in this Advent season to get ready for the King who is coming.

But like the Hebrews of old, we can dismiss this hope as something in the far distant future — something like a new branch that will take years and years to grow into a strong and powerful limb. I once got a birthday card that showed a man carrying a big sign that said, "Repent." But when you opened the card, it read: "Repent, but do it tomorrow . . . today's your birthday so have a ball." Repent yes, but there is no hurry. The Lord's new king won't be coming for years and years!

I wonder if it is not our human tendency to push hope into some far distant future that causes us to miss the fulfillment of so many of God's great promises to us. So often God's answers to our cries for help and deliverance come in a form we could never imagine. In Copenhagen, Denmark, there is a statue of Christ that pictures our Lord with his arms outstretched in love and compassion. For many years it has moved people to tears who stand before this figure of the Christ that seems to beckon us to come to him. What is strange about the sculpture is that its creator, Bertel Thorwaldsen, intended to create a very different kind of figure. His original model was a massive clay figure of Jesus as a hero king. The head was thrown back imperiously, and the hands of Jesus were raised as if in a gesture of command. The great Danish sculptor finished his work and then left the statue to dry in his studio overnight. But the sea mists and fog came in that night and worked a strange change in the artist's handiwork. When the sculptor returned, he found the head of Christ fallen forward and the hands outstretched in a gesture of love and entreaty. In his heart Thorwaldsen knew what words he would place in the inscription beneath the statue: "Come unto me, all that are heavy laden, and I will give you rest."

The hope which Isaiah envisioned so long ago comes to us in ways we never dreamed possible as the Living Christ enters our lives and turns our despair into newness of life.

2. A Message Of Peace And Justice

Isaiah's message from God not only brings the hope of a new order, but a description of a world where justice rules, and where the whole creation lives in peace and harmony. In all of scripture, you cannot find a picture more idyllic than this one! Who of us can even imagine a world where the wild beasts and little children play together and where the earth is full of the knowledge of the Lord!

And that's our problem! We tend to dismiss such a picture as an idealistic utopia, an impossible dream shared by a few sentimental environmentalists but not something we can ever imagine happening on our earth. We have our own methods of dealing with wild beasts. The high-powered rifle is our answer and that is just one more evidence of how we identify a golden age to come with materialism and our own achievement and power. Our visions of a peaceful age are based on greater prosperity, more government services, no unemployment and more of the good life for everyone.

But Isaiah's vision of justice and peace is much more than some human effort to reorder the society. It is based not only on changing the structures of the society but on changing human hearts so that they will be "full of the knowledge of the Lord as the waters cover the sea." God's Christmas message has always been about peace on earth and good will among people, but it finds its genesis in Jesus' demand that we seek first the kingdom of God and all these other things shall be added.

Our difficulty in catching hold of Isaiah's vision of peace may rest in our misunderstanding of what the peace of God really is. Some years ago an art contest was held in a Maine seacoast town. Local artists were invited to submit a painting that portrayed the idea of peace. Many entries depicted beautiful idyllic scenes of peaceful landscapes and gentle waters lapping against the shore. But the picture which took first prize showed a rocky seacoast in the midst of a violent storm. Waves were crashing against the rocks sending the sprays of water high into the air. On the surface of it, the scene was anything but peaceful! However, a closer examination of the painting showed a sea gull, just a tiny bird, huddled in a cleft in the rock. All around the bird, the angry sea pounded on the seacoast, but the little gull shielded by the rock, was safe and secure in the midst of the storm.

That is much closer to the Bible's understanding of peace — not an absence of conflict, but a sustaining presence within our troubled lives that keeps us safe and secure in the midst of the turbulance. God's Christmas message to you and to me is that we can know that peace through the presence of our Lord in our daily lives. A year ago I found myself in a crowded mall on the day before Christmas, doing the shopping I should have done weeks before. It was a terrible place with wall to wall people all pushing and shoving their way to the check out counter. When I finally got in line, I wondered to myself if I would even make it to the cash register before Christmas! But suddenly in the midst of all my anxious worry, I had the unmistakable feeling that someone was watching me. I turned around and there right behind me was a beautiful baby boy with large blue eyes staring at me. The child was held safely in his mother's arms and in the midst of all the noise and confusion of the world around us, this child waited with a calmness and quietness that seemed to say to me, "What's the matter with you? Haven't you got anyone to take care of you like I do?" It was a humbling moment, but one in which I learned more about the peace that Christ promises than I have in a very long time.

Isaiah's vision of a world where peace and justice are possible is based on that same conviction that it is God who brings us peace. Isaiah never forgot that this is still God's world, and that one day God will be triumphant over everything that is evil and oppressive in our world. Isaiah could envision a

19

reconciliation that would not only include human beings and the Living God, but even the animal kingdom and all of nature. In Jesus Christ our broken, troubled world catches a glimpse of a time to come when the earth shall be full of the knowledge of the Lord. In the midst of wars and rumors of wars, we need not despair. God is already at work through the power of suffering love to bring about that new age, and every now and then, you and I are privileged to see God at work.

A pastor who touched my life in a very significant way lost an eye during the Second World War. He ended up being taken prisoner on Christmas Eve by German forces. Taken to a field hospital, it seemed as if nothing could ease the terrible pain in his eye, nor the empty loneliness he felt in his heart. It was Christmas Eve, but there was no peace on earth. He lay in the midst of wounded, dying men wondering if he would even see another Christmas Day.

And then a hand reached out from the cot next to his, and a wounded German soldier tried to say something to him. He could not understand the words, but suddenly he realized that the German was singing. In a voice filled with the anguish of his own pain, this German was singing the words, "Silent night, holy night, all is calm, all is bright." Slowly those patients who could, began to sing as well, and before long the guards, the doctors and the nurses lifted up their voices in praise to the Christ Child, the Prince of Peace. It was one of those incredible moments when like Isaiah of old, we can glimpse a world where the power of God's love is greater than human hatred.

That message of hope and of peace is God's Christmas greeting to you and to me. It's a message of good news to a world often filled with bad news. More than that, it's a Christmas message that can change your life!

Christmas Preparations We Often Forget

It does not seem to bother the children that Christmas is so close. Why is it they never seem to have any trouble getting ready for it? We older and wiser ones make a much harder thing of it; we always insist there is so much to do to get ready. Perhaps the difference is that the children are content to let Christmas happen, while we are so sure that it can't happen unless we do all the right things to make it happen.

Many of the things we do to adorn this season, to set the stage for the drama that is coming, are certainly good, and belong there — so long as they do not take over so completely that we have no time or room for that other kind of preparation, which is nothing more nor less than being ready, like the children, to let Christmas happen in its own way. Or perhaps we should say, to let it happen in God's own way!

There is a comparison to be drawn here with the kind of preparation that God urged upon people of old before Christmas happened the first time. Isaiah offers us a somewhat different perspective on the kinds of preparations we ought to be making for the coming of Christ. Isaiah speaks in this passage of three very different promises that God will fulfill in the coming of Jesus Christ into our world.

1. The Promise Of Judgment

The first promise may sound somewhat strange to our ears because it is the promise of judgment that Christ's coming will bring to the world. "Behold, your God will come with vengeance, with the recompense of God." As the ancient prophets looked forward to the Messiah's entrance into the world, they saw something we often miss — that the Christ of Bethlehem is the same Christ who comes to judge the earth and to live and reign forever and ever. We cannot ignore the judgment of Christmas. There is an imminent judgment right there in Christ's birth, a judgment that goes hand in hand with our Lord's coming to be the bringer of salvation.

It is illustrated, perhaps, in the story that has been told of the shipwreck survivor cast up on an uninhabited island. For days, months and years he waited for rescue. He watched from the island's heights for a ship, but none came. Then, one day, on the distant horizon, he saw it: first a sail, then a ship coming closer and closer. He thrilled at the prospect of being rescued at last. But when the ship dropped anchor off-shore, and a landing party approached the beach, he was afraid, after all this time of aloneness, to meet his own kind face to face. He hid himself. The men of the landing party saw signs of his presence. They called. They searched. But he knew the island too well and eluded their every effort to find him. At day's end, they left, and as he watched the ship sail away out of his sight, he fell down on the sand of his island prison and wept.

The judgment of Christmas is like that. It comes, Christ comes, to rescue and to save us. But we can hide from all that if we choose. We know the hiding places in our lives well enough to keep from ever meeting the Child of Bethlehem. We can watch from the safety of our busy preparations as the Christmas event comes and then passes on. And we may well weep for having rejected its hope when Christmas is past, for as Jesus himself once said, "This is the judgment — that light has entered the world and men have preferred darkness to light (John 3:19, Phillips version)."

Isaiah foretold the coming glory and majesty of the Lord, but he knew that any such coming brings with it a judgment. If we choose to stay hidden in our preferred darkness, we may well discover to our sorrow what the judgment of Christmas is all about.

2. The Promise Of Exciting Changes

But happily Isaiah could see in the promise of the Messiah's coming other preparations that would bring joy to the hearts of people. This passage describes the promise of exciting changes that will take place in the world. When God comes into the world, there will be a revolutionary newness to things, a shifting from the status quo to a whole new order of life. Just listen as Isaiah describes a few of those exciting changes: "the eyes of the blind shall be opened, and the ears of the deaf unstopped; then shall the lame man leap like a hart, and the tongue of the dumb sing for joy." Christmas does change things, doesn't it? It changes the looks of our homes and our community. It changes our stores and our city streets, our highways and our air terminals. It changes the pattern of life from dull routine to excited anticipation. And of course, it changes things like our bank balance and perhaps even our waistlines! Sometimes it even changes our attitudes just a bit. For at least a few weeks, there seems to be a touch of goodwill that is not felt in other seasons of the year.

Now these exciting changes are fine as far as they go, but the exciting changes Isaiah foretold run much deeper. They are changes that strike at the very roots of life, and changes that go well beyond the Christmas season. What Isaiah is trying to describe is the simple fact that since Jesus Christ entered our world, nothing has ever been the same again. Our relationship with God is different. Our call to be a part of Christ's mission in the world is different. Our understanding of what is truly lasting and important is different. The world has never quite been the same place since God's Messiah came among us.

There is an old Christmas story that reminds us of what our world would be like if Jesus Christ had not come. It is about a little boy on Christmas Eve who hurriedly checks his stocking by the mantle and the beautiful Christmas tree in the living room before going to bed. He was so very excited, but it seemed as if he had not been asleep for long when a rather harsh voice shouted, "Get up." Remembering that it should be Christmas morning, the boy bounded out of bed, pulled on his clothes and hurried downstairs. What a shock awaited him! No stocking hung from the mantel. There was no tree with presents beneath it. His parents were nowhere to be seen. Everything instead had a dull drab look about it. The little lad went to the door and was startled to hear the whistle from the local factory blowing its shrill call to work. "What's the plant doing open on Christmas day?" he wondered. Then he looked down the street. There were no wreaths on the doors, no bright lights in front of the homes. Instead all the shops were open for business as usual. He hurried towards the center of town. "Why are all the stores open on Christmas?" he asked a woman he passed on the street. "Christmas," she muttered, "I've never heard of it!" Everywhere it was the same. People hurried by and no one even stopped to greet the now fearful boy.

Suddenly, he knew there was one place he could go where people knew about Christmas — his church! The boy and his family always went to the Christmas Day service in the little church. He hurried as fast as he could along the street, but when he came to where the church should have stood, there was only a vacant lot filled with tall weeds and debris. He thought of his school, but when he ran to the corner where it had stood, there was another vacant lot! The same he soon discovered was true of where the town library he loved had once stood and the YMCA where he played basketball. It was then that the sorrowful boy heard a low moan. Looking down, he saw a man lying on the snow, obviously hurt. "A car hit me an hour ago," stammered the man, "and no one will help me! Please get some help!" In desperation the boy decided he could run to the hospital just a few blocks away and get help. But even as he reached the street where Good Samaritan Hospital had stood, he began to see another vacant lot, this time with an ugly concrete wall around it. No hospital! No church! No school! No Christmas!

In an agony of spirit the little boy stumbled toward his home. The previous night his father had read from the family Bible the wonderful story of the Savior's birth. As he entered the house, there was the Bible still by his father's chair in the living room. He opened it eagerly, but where the New Testament should have been, there was only a series of empty pages. Across one of the pages, someone had written the words, "If Only Jesus Christ Had Come." The boy raced upstairs and flung himself on his bed, crying softly for a world that simply was no more.

Then he heard his mother's voice saying excitedly, "Bobby get up. It's Christmas morning!" The little lad sprang from his bed and ran to the window. Out there on the houses were the beautiful wreaths! Brightly lit Christmas trees could be seen up and down the street, and as he listened, he heard the chimes playing from the church bell tower, "Joy to the World, The Lord has Come." "You did come," he whispered, "thank you Jesus for coming to our world!"[1] Perhaps it is only a children's story, but it helps remind us of the truth Isaiah could see so clearly: the coming of the Christ means exciting changes — changes in us and in our world that will last long after Christmas is past.

3. The Promise Of Togetherness

Christmas judgment and Christmas changes and now one more reality that Isaiah hoped to prepare us for: Christmas togetherness. "The ransomed of the Lord shall return and come to Zion with singing; they shall obtain joy and gladness and sorrow and sighing shall flee away." It is almost as if Isaiah could foresee a drawing together of people, a coming home

25

again, a time when the walls that divide us would be taken down, and the people of the world would know a harmony and togetherness never known before.

Now perhaps you are saying, "What's so unusual about that?" All kinds of people come home for Christmas. We have declared a cease fire in our wars for Christmas! Isn't that quite naturally what happens in the world at Christmastime? But Isaiah would be quick to tell us that what he is talking about is much more than a simple homecoming or a cessation of hostilities. Isaiah could foresee what is so often missing in our lives all year long — a peace with God and with one another that is so desperately needed in our world.

How often all our feverishness and scurrying about before Christmas and during the holidays really serves to keep us apart rather than truly bringing us together. Perhaps you recall that one home where on a hectic night-before-Christmas the father was busy with bundles and chores and upset over the bills. Mother's nerves were frayed. The litte daughter was constantly in the way, no matter what she did. Finally she was sent off to bed with some harsh words and a hasty "Good Night." As she prayed the Lord's Prayer alone before going to sleep, the high-pitched tension of the day took its toll; her mind was a little mixed up when she came to the middle of the prayer and said, "And forgive us our Christmases, as we forgive those who Christmas against us."

"Forgive us our Christmases!" How many of us need to pray that prayer! For all too often we let the madness we inject into Christmas drive us further apart instead of letting the peace of Christmas draw us together in a whole new way. Christmas togetherness is not something we manufacture within ourselves. It is God's wondrous gift that turns our hearts outward toward one another. It is God who breaks down all that divides us from one another — even our crazy Christmas celebrations — and finally brings us the true joy of the Lord's grace and mercy and love.

When I think of the power of Christmas to bring us together, I remember a true story written by actor David Niven about his experience on Christmas Eve 1939. He had just arrived in England from Hollywood to volunteer for the British Army. Having had previous military experience, Niven was commissioned a second lieutenant and given a command of a platoon. The group was sent to France and no one was very happy about what was then called "the phony war" or having to be away from friends and family at Christmas. Even worse for the men of this unit was the irritating fact that they were commanded by a Hollywood actor! As David Niven wrote, "the men were not mutinous — but they were certainly 40 of the least well-disposed characters I ever have been associated with, let alone been in command of."

No leave was permitted on Christmas Eve because the unit might well see action the next day. The entire platoon was billeted in the shabby stables of a country farm. Now it so happened that David Niven every night of his life took the moment before going to bed to kneel down and offer a simple prayer to God. But that night he was faced with a difficult decision. If he suddenly knelt down in prayer here in front of an already hostile group of men, wouldn't those already disgruntled soldiers see that as just one more act of Hollywood flamboyance? On the other hand, Niven had been thinking all day about the Christ's coming into the world, and his heart simply would not let him go to bed without thanking God for that wondrous gift. Summoning up his courage, he knelt down there in the barn and began to pray quietly. There was some snickering at first, but it soon died away. When he finished, Niven lay down on the straw and looked rather sheepishly around the stable where he saw every man in the unit on his knees in prayer. It was not the first time that God entered a stable — and touched the hearts of people with peace and togetherness.[2]

Those are the realities that Isaiah could see in the coming of the Messiah: Christmas judgment, Christmas changes and Christmas togetherness. As you prepare once more for the Lord's coming, be sure you make time for the realities in Christmas that can change your life now and for all time!

27

The Baby Who Changes Everything

There was a commotion in Roaring Camp. Cherokee Sal, the only woman in this rough, tough mining settlement, was dead after giving birth to a son whose father was unknown. Around the crude cabin where the newborn child lay helpless and crying, the hundred or so hard-bitten goldrush miners gathered in curiosity and concern. Death was so common here, but birth — this was a whole new experience.

Stumpy, a fugitive from justice on charges of bigamy, had by common consent taken charge of the little one's arrival. Shortly he allowed the miners to view the new baby, suggesting that it would be appropriate to make a contribution for the helpless orphan. So they came filing in, unconsciously taking off their hats in the presence of this miracle of new life, and putting their gifts at his side — a revolver, a diamond ring, a sling shot and a silver spoon. But now what to do?

The next day the inhabitants of Roaring Camp met in serious deliberation, and without the usual slugging and brawling, decided that working together they would all help raise this child. Stumpy was designated the particular guardian with a female mule as his first assistant. Strange to say, the little one thrived under their care, and equally strange was the effect on Roaring Camp. The little infant was named "Tommy

Luck." His cabin, a filthy mess before he had been born there, was scrupulously cleaned, whitewashed and fixed up. A cradle was packed in by mule, and that made all the rest of the makeshift furniture so shabby in contrast that by common consensus, the whole place had to be done over.

In turn the local gambling joint and bar, the so-called grocery store, had to be spruced up to be in keeping with the Luck's cabin, and before long, the remainder of the settlement followed suit. This, and Stumpy's remarkable but understandable refusal to let anybody hold the Luck unless he was spotlessly clean, shaven and shorn, produced miracles in the miners' appearances. And equally amazing was the change in their conduct. Shouting within sound of Tommy's cabin was forbidden, lest he be wakened, and shortly the usual profanity was practically given up as not right for their boy to hear. From being Roaring Camp, the ugly drunken frontier settlement became, as one Cockney criminal inhabitant expressed it, "kind of 'eavenly." There was talk of further improvement and even of inviting some decent families to live there to benefit Tommy Luck with their presence. Word got around to the outside world of this miracle of change through the pony express riders who would say, "They've a street up there in Roaring Camp that's better than any street in Red Dog. They've got vines and flowers round their cabins, and they wash themselves twice a day . . . and they sure worship an Injun baby."

A baby — a baby who changed life! Bret Harte's memorable short story was never intended to be a Christmas story, but it nonetheless is a parable that can help us understand God's dealing with us in Jesus Christ. It has been said that when a wrong wants righting, or a truth wants presenting, or a continent wants opening, God sends a baby into the world to do it. People may think that the course of the world is ultimately determined by big battalions, decisive battles and all the panoply of power, but all the while God is setting it, quietly, in littleness and in weakness, through the birth of a child. For example back in 1809, Napoleon stood over much of the western world like a Colossus. From Spain to the Near East, kings and popes did his bidding or suffered the consequences. Nations and peoples trembled at the menace of his might. People were impressed with his power and acknowledged him as the world shaper of his time. No one paid any attention to the cries of newborn babies amidst the cries of battle and the clamor of war.

But in the same year of 1809 there was born in a crude cabin in Kentucky a child who was named Abraham Lincoln. And in Massachusetts, a baby called Oliver Wendell Holmes came into the world. In Liverpool another baby was born by the name of William Gladstone, while in Somersby, Alfred Tennyson was coming to birth. In Germany, Felix Mendelssohn was born that year, and in Poland, Louis Braille. And so they came into the world from the hand of God, these and countless other babies, including Cyrus McCormick and Charles Darwin. Within six years, Napoleon was through and his empire shattered, but Lincoln's words, Tennyson's poetry, and Braille's humanitarianism, McCormick's invention, Gladstone's vision and Darwin's ideas are still bearing fruit and reaching more lives than ever before. "When a wrong wants righting, or a truth wants presenting, or a continent wants opening, God sends a baby into the world to do it."

So we come to Isaiah's words, "Behold a young woman shall conceive and bear a son, and shall call his name "Emmanuel." Isaiah foretold the birth of a child as a sign to King Ahaz of Judah that God would deliver his nation from the treachery of Syria and Israel. The name, Emmanuel, of course means "God with us." As modern scholars are quick to point out, the words of Isaiah may have had a much more immediate fulfillment in King Ahaz's time with the birth of a baby that signaled the defeat of Judah's enemies. However, in the minds of Christian believers through the centuries, Isaiah's words have come to symbolize the far greater deliverance God sent into this world with the birth of our Lord Jesus Christ whom the disciples knew as Emmanuel. God with us now! Once again, God chose what is low and despised in the world to bring to naught the things that are. As John Buchan has written,

"There in Judea was born the One who was to proclaim a kingdom mightier than Rome and a world saved not by a man who became God, but by a God who became a man for our sakes."

This One who began life on earth as the baby of Bethlehem changed life so that it has never been the same since. Sometimes in our cynicism, we listen to the news reports of bloodshed, crime, disease, destruction, brokenness and hostility, and conclude that the world around us is beyond saving. I love the story of the shipwrecked sailor who had spent three years on a tiny island. He was elated when he finally spied a boat approaching his island prison, but as the boat neared the shore where he was waiting, a young naval officer tossed the distraught sailor a bundle of old newspapers. "Captain's compliments," he shouted. "Read these newspapers and then let us know if you still want to be rescued!" We know that the world we live in today is filled with misery and suffering, hatred and hostility, but we must never forget the radical changes that the Babe of Bethlehem, God's Emmanuel, have begun in our poor old world.

1. Radical Changes In Our Outer World

Think for a few moments of the things that are different because God once came into our world in Jesus Christ. No longer, for instance, are women regarded as men's possessions without a soul of their own. Jesus changed all that by showing a graciousness and esteem to women unknown in the world before he came. No longer are children maltreated as of old, or babies cast out to die. Children became precious when he said, "Let the little ones come to me, for of such is the kingdom of God." No longer is it accepted that some human beings are born to be slaves and others to be masters, since Jesus died for all to deliver us from the bondage of sin. No longer are some races regarded as inferior to others, because the Christ calls us to "love one another as I have loved you." Human life took on a new dignity and worth when he told us, "The very hairs of your head are numbered." Jesus lifted family life to new and glorious heights when he exalted purity and faithfulness within the marriage bond. He stimulated learning to new purpose and depth when he promised, "You shall know the truth, and the truth shall make you free." Labor is no longer scorned as something lowly since he became the carpenter of Nazareth and the servant of all. Hospitals and homes for the elderly, playgrounds and libraries, and institutions dedicated to public service all draw their being from the source of his compassion and concern. The powerful and noble concepts that motivate our lives at their best, freedom and peace, decency and kindness, forgiveness and love, all these we have drawn from Emmanuel. Of course, all these things did not happen at once, and much remains to be realized in our world as Christ continues to challenge us over the problems of war and race, economic injustice and the source of AIDS. But let us never forget that the One who began life as a baby in Bethlehem is the one who has changed all things!

Kenneth Scott Latourette, the distinguished Yale historian once wrote, "Measured by its fruits in the human race, that short life of Jesus has been the most influential ever lived on this planet. Gauged by the consequences which have followed his life, Jesus of Nazareth is central in the human story and the most important event in the history of our world."

2. The Possibility Of Inner Change

The outward changes in society are the evidences of a far more important kind of change that Emmanuel, Jesus the Christ has made possible in his coming. Because God came to be with us in that little child in the manger, our human weakness and insufficiency under the demands of life have been caught up in the all-sufficiency and gracious power of the eternal Creator. We have discovered in Christ how much God loves us, and with God's help, how much of life can be changed. Jesus never eliminated the qualities that made Peter Peter or Paul Paul. Peter's impetuosity and Paul's imperturbable drive were still there after Christ had touched them, but you would have to look twice to be sure it was the same life. So every generation testifies to the transforming power of Emmanuel in our inward lives: Augustine was a frivolous libertine until Jesus changed his inner spirit and brought forth a spiritual giant. Francis of Assisi was a self-seeking dilettante when Christ changed him into a self-sacrificing servant of the needy and warm-hearted lover of nature. In our own times it has been Emmanuel's touch upon people like singer Ethel Waters, atomic scientist William Pollard, onetime agnostic C. S. Lewis and writer Dorothy Day that has made a radical difference in the lives of people. It is Jesus who has brought healing and wholeness, forgiveness and restoration to countless women and men, and who comes once more so that we may experience in our lives the lilt and the luster, the glory and the gladness that God intends for creation.

Pete Richards was the loneliest man in the town on the day little Jean opened the door of his shop. The store window was filled with a disarray of old-fashioned things: bracelets and lockets, gold rings and silver boxes, images of jade and ivory porcelain figurines. On this winter's afternoon just before Christmas, little Jean had spent a long time with her forehead pressed against the glass, looking for something quite special. Finally, with a satisfied air, she entered Pete Richards' store. "Mister," she began, "could I have that string of blue beads in the window?" Pete brought them out. She looked at them and said, "They're perfect! Will you wrap them up pretty for me, please?"

Pete studied her with a somewhat stony air. "Are you buying these for someone?" "They're for my big sister. She takes care of me. This will be the first Christmas since my mom died and I want to do something special for my sister." "How much money do you have?" asked Pete warily. Little Jean opened a handkerchief and poured out a pile of pennies on the counter. "I emptied my bank," she explained simply. "It's everything I have."

Pete Richards looked at the child thoughtfully. How could he tell her that it cost many times what she had in money to buy it? And as he looked at the little girl with the trusting look in her blue eyes, something deep within Pete Richards began to come back to life. He looked at her wheat colored hair and her sea blue eyes, and remembered another woman with that same yellow in her hair and with eyes just as blue. The turquoise necklace had been hers. But there had come a rainy night — a truck skidding on a slippery road — and the life was crushed out of his dream. Since then, Pete Richards had lived with grief and bitterness and an emptiness in his soul that until this little girl had come into his shop, he had carefully buried from the eyes of the world. The blue eyes of little Jean jolted him into acute remembrance of what he had lost. Carefully he wrapped the blue beads in scarlet paper and tied the package with a bright green ribbon. "There you are," he said. "Don't lose it on the way home."

The next few days were busy ones for Pete Richards as many customers finished their Christmas shopping. He was just about to lock the door of his shop on Christmas Eve when a woman hurried in. With an inexplicable start, Pete realized she looked familiar, yet he could not imagine having seen her before. Her hair was golden and her eyes were blue. Without speaking, she drew a package from her purse and asked, "Did this necklace come from your shop?" "Yes," said Pete, "they came from this shop." "Then I must return them, because I am sure my little sister did not have enough money to pay for them."

Pete Richards looked at the woman for a long time and then said, "The price is always confidential between the seller and the customer. The little girl who purchased this necklace paid the biggest price anyone can ever pay. She gave all she had. What's more, she helped me remember the One who gave his life on a cross, so that we might all live."[1]

The One who changes all things can change you and me for the best, if we will open our hearts to meet him. As a photographic plate exposed to light bears the image of that reflected

35

light upon it and so is changed, you and I, open, sensitive, receptive can face the light of Jesus Christ until God's own likeness is imprinted on our souls. This is the deliverance foretold so long ago by the prophet Isaiah in the coming of Emmanuel, God with us now!

"O holy child of Bethlehem, descend to us, we pray,
Cast out our sin and enter in, be born in us today.
We hear the Christmas angels the great glad tidings tell;
O come to us, abide with us, our Lord Emmanuel."

What Christmas Is About

Charlie Brown isn't the only one who asks, "What's Christmas all about?" Real people also ask that same question. Several years ago there was an exchange student from Indonesia, spending his first December in America. The crowds of shoppers in the stores, the Santa Clauses, the bright lights, the trees, the manger scenes, the parties, and the growing sense of excitement and revelry — it was all more than a little confusing to him. Then one night as he sat watching television with his host family, the announcer insisted that Bud Light was the only proper thing to serve your holiday guests. The young man with a puzzled expression turned and said to his American hosts, "What's Christmas all about, anyway? I just don't understand!"

Now we could answer that young man by saying, "Christmas is the church's celebration of the birth of God's Son, Jesus Christ." But then, how do we explain the reindeer, the tinsel, and the Bud Light? Our problem, of course, is the simple fact that with so many people changing, refashioning and adapting the holiest of days for their own use and profit, it's easy for God's people to forget what Christmas is really about.

There are some words spoken long ago by the Prophet Isaiah that can help us grasp afresh the wonder of Jesus Christ

37

coming into our world. Isaiah, when he first spoke these words could never have fully imagined a Messiah like Jesus Christ. But down through the long centuries, God's people have looked back to the names Isaiah chose to describe the hope of Israel — names like Wonderful Counselor, Mighty God, Everlasting Father, Prince of Peace — and felt those names perfectly fit the one who entered life in a Bethlehem stable. So let us look afresh at each of those names that we might understand who Jesus is and what Jesus has done for us.

1. Wonderful Counselor

The first name is Wonderful Counselor. In the King James Version, there is a comma between Wonderful and Counselor. It ought not to be there. It is a phrase, these two words, Wonderful Counselor. Now a counselor is somebody who is supposed to have some kind of expertise — the ability to help. If we ever seek out a counselor, we must go to that person in the faith that he or she knows his or her business, and more importantly, knows how to help us. When we speak of the God we know in Jesus Christ as a Wonderful Counselor, we are saying that we believe in a God who knows what we need, and knows best how to help us live life in this world.

On that first Christmas, it must not have seemed that way at all! The people had expected God to come as a military Messiah, strong and mighty. Instead God came as a tiny helpless baby boy. They had expected a Messiah to enter the world with great fanfare, but instead some angels sang to some shepherds and that was about it! The Messiah that God sent was definitely not what people expected, but a wise God knew that Jesus is exactly what people needed in our human lives, and the name Wonderful Counselor, forces each of us to ask afresh, "Do we trust God? Do we honestly believe that God knows what we need and what is best for us?"

There is a Dutch fable that tells about some tulip bulbs in the bulb bin. These three bulbs were meditating on the meaning of life and how to get the most out of it. One of the tulip bulbs whose name was "No" said, "I don't believe there is anything more to life than what I have already experienced. I'm pretty well satisfied with the way my life is. I'm just going to stay over here in my corner and be happy." There was another bulb named "Maybe." This bulb said, "I'm not too sure. I think there is more to life than what I have experienced. I feel a desire to know more and find more, and it's all up to me to find what else there is." So this bulb squeezed and finally in frustration, shriveled away into a corner. A third bulb was named "Yes." This bulb said, "I hear there is more to life than we know, but that on our own, we can't find anything. What we have to do is put ourselves in the hands of the Lord, and with God's help, we will find it." Just then a hand reached down into the bulb bin. "No" hid in the corner. "Maybe" shriveled away, but "Yes" willingly put himself into the hand. The little bulb was buried in the ground through the long winter, but in the spring the bulb burst forth into a new and wondrous life.

Those same choices are given to every one of us. We can say there is nothing more to life than what we have seen. We can attempt to find life in all its fullness out of our own strength and effort, or we can realize that no one finds life eternal alone, but that life begins when we depend on someone beyond ourselves. That someone has a name. The name is Jesus Christ, God's Wonderful Counselor. If we put our trust in Jesus Christ, we can make our way through life.

2. Mighty God

But let us turn to another of the names Isaiah used for the one who would come to deliver Israel. The words, Mighty God, literally could be translated "Conquering Warrior." It carries the idea that God will be victorious over all enemies. No one will be able to defeat God. But as we look at the world in which we live, it certainly does not seem as if the enemies

39

of the Living God have been defeated! If anything, it seems as if all that is evil, and violent, and godless, is winning big! Mighty God? It does not seem like it. That first Christmas is a good example. If God is so mighty, why did poor Mary and Joseph have to make that long, agonizing trip to Bethlehem to be taxed? If God is so mighty, why did God allow the Roman Empire to oppress people in this way? And why was there no room at the Inn? Why didn't God just clear out the people so that Jesus would have a room in which to be born?

Those are real questions, but perhaps we have misunderstood what is meant by the name "Mighty." When we talk about the power of God, we often think in terms of raw brute force. Maybe that is not the way God chooses to be powerful. Maybe God chooses to show power in a different way. Perhaps the power of God is best seen not in what the world calls strength and force, but in the weakness and vulnerability of love. Many years ago there was a popular movie, *How Green Was My Valley*. Roddy McDowell played the part of a boy who was different from the rest of the kids in school, and was picked on and bullied by everyone, including the teacher. One day after a particularly bad beating in front of all the students by the teacher, the boy's older brother came to school and beat the teacher to a pulp. Everybody at first felt good. Justice had been done. The evil had been avenged. But slowly, the people in that Valley remembered how Jesus had taught that nothing is ever solved by repaying evil for evil. The ultimate way to stop evil is not by force but by courageous love. It is by a cross lifted up to the heavens, when with all the chance in the world to revile back, Jesus dies with a prayer of love upon his lips.

This power of love is a strange power, but in Jesus Christ, we begin to grasp the awesome power of God that is often strongest in our lives when it appears to be the weakest. Golfer Gary Player has long been a deeply committed Christian. Playing in a tournament in Dayton, Ohio, Gary came to the 10th green. As he was walking up to the green, a man suddenly came out of the crowd and threw a glassful of soft drink in the golfer's face. Now Player is a very muscular person. He had a golf club in his hand, and it would have been so easy, so tempting to just knock this attacker to the ground. Instead, Player looked at the man and said, simply, "Sir, what did I ever do to you?" There was a long pause, and the man ashamedly walked away. Player picked up his club, wiped himself off, and promptly sunk the ball into the cup. How could he do that? How could he return good for evil? The power of Jesus Christ, our Mighty God, is the power to love, and Christmas is a reminder that God's love will ultimately triumph over every evil and every wrong in this world.

3. Everlasting Father

Isaiah used a third name for the one who was to deliver Israel — the name Everlasting Father. That term literally means, "one who constantly cares for his children." Please understand that we are talking about an ideal father who truly loves children. There are some fathers who can in no way be compared to God for they are unloving, selfish and insensitive. But when Jesus called God, "Father," Jesus was describing a very personal, intimate relationship with a parent whose love is personal and whose care is constant. Christmas was God's way of showing the world how much God loves, and how far the love of God will go to reach our hearts.

One of the Peanuts characters made the statement, "I love humanity. It's people I can't stand!" A lot of us have that problem when it comes to loving, but the Christ of Christmas reveals a God whose love is personal, unconditional and endless. Think of the variety of human beings who came to the Bethlehem manger that night so long ago — lowly shepherds from out of a Bethlehem field, wise men who were among the most respected persons of their day, and a couple of peasants named Mary and Joseph. Christ came to the up and in as well as to the down and out, and to them all, Jesus said, "God loves you."

Do we grasp the wonder of what it is like to be loved with no strings attached? I recall a friend telling about a family

41

named Adams that he knew. Mrs. Adams was considered by her neighbors to be the weakest woman they knew. Today we would call her a "wimp." She was considered weak because she continued to live with a worthless husband who failed to provide for her necessities, a man whose badge was his bottle and his debts. Mrs. Adams had lived for years accepting the cruelty of her critical neighbors and her husband's cruelty. When he came home drunk, she would put him to bed, care for him and continue her efforts to get him some help. One day a newcomer to the neighborhood asked this woman why she continued to live with her husband. "It seems," said the neighbor, "as if he never says a kind word to you, never even treats you as a human being." With a knowing smile, Mrs. Adams responded, "I know what you say is true, but he wasn't always like that. The simple truth is, I still love him and cannot picture my life without him."

How much more God loves us. The name, Everlasting Father, is the good news that God's love is personal, unconditional and endless.

4. Prince Of Peace

Isaiah's fourth name for the one who would deliver Israel was the Prince of Peace. Surely this term takes us to the heart of what Christmas is about. What could be more peaceful than that beautiful scene of a holy night, with shepherds watching and angels singing, and Mary placing the baby in Bethlehem's stable? But Christmas is much more than a sentimental remembrance of the birth of a baby long ago. Christmas is about God's plan for peace on this earth, and as another Christmas breaks on our not-so-peaceful world, we are challenged once more to ask ourselves what we have done in the past year to bring God's peace into the lives of people around us.

For Christmas is about a world at war with itself. Christmas is about the need for God in the midst of bombings, riots, missiles screaming down-range to their pinpointed targets, murders, barroom brawls, domestic violence and drunken family arguments. The Word became flesh, not to give us some sentimental recollection of a long-ago and far-away picture of peace, but to live among us. Christ came to live among us as the Prince of Peace. Christ came to give us the hope, and the way to find an everlasting ceasefire on this earth. Christ came to bring to fulfillment, in one way or another, the ancient prophecies which say of him, "He makes wars to cease. He breaks the bow, and cuts the spear in two. He burns the war chariot. And men shall beat their swords into plowshares, and their spears into pruning hooks; neither shall they learn war anymore." Christ was born for this — for our peacelessness.

There is an ancient legend which says that when the Child of Bethlehem was taken from the manger, no cow or donkey or sheep or goat would eat the hay left there where he had been cradled. And when the stable boy wondered why, he discovered that the wisps of hay had turned to gold. It is only a legend, but this much is parable enough to tell us that where Christ enters in — in those hearts where he finds room to be born — everything changes, and the peace with God and with one another we so need becomes God's gift to us. By the grace of God, it can happen to us.

Christmas 1
Isaiah 63:7-9

What Is God Like?

There is an old story about a little girl who was one day drawing a picture. She was so engrossed in her work that her mother asked, "What are you drawing?" "Oh, it's a picture of God," said the youngster. "A picture of God?" "Darling, no one knows what God looks like!" "No," said the little girl, "but they will when I get through." What is God like? How can I find God? These are questions that men and women have asked across the centuries and still ask today. In some inspired words, the prophet Isaiah gives us a portrait of what God is like. Like the little child drawing her picture, Isaiah could not capture all the fullness of the person of the Living God, but his words have come down to us not only as a high moment in the understanding of the ancient Hebrews, but as a wondrous description of the God revealed in Jesus Christ.

1. A God Of Steadfast Love

Isaiah's word portrait begins with a God of Steadfast Love. "I will recount the steadfast love of the Lord . . ." wrote Isaiah, and later in this same passage, he refers to "the abundance of God's steadfast love." Somebody once pointed out the difference between generosity and compassion. Generosity is when you bake two pies for the annual church bazaar, and compassion is when you buy those same pies back after they failed to sell! Compassion is a truly wonderful quality, but the steadfast love of which Isaiah speaks is something that goes far beyond ordinary human kindness and love. Steadfast love is a love that knows no limits. It is a love that nothing can ever change. It is a love so strong that not even death, said the Apostle Paul in his letter to the Romans, can ever separate us from it.

But how do we know that God's love for us is like that? In most cases, love is expressed in giving to the one who is loved. That's why we have just exchanged gifts with those whom we love. Giving a gift is a way to tell someone how much we love them, care about them or appreciate them. Unfortunately, at least in America, our Christmas celebrations have moved from being a time for adoration to a time for accumulation! However, the real proof of love is not in the material gift itself. It is the person in the gift. It is how much of yourself is given that really reveals the depths of love in your heart for another.

There is a lovely Christmas story that helps us understand this truth in a simple way. An African boy listened carefully as the teacher explained why it is that Christians give presents to each other on Christmas Day. "The gift is an expression of our joy over the birth of Jesus and our friendship for each other," she said. When Christmas day came, the boy brought the teacher a sea shell of lustrous beauty. "Where did you ever find such a beautiful shell?" the teacher asked as she gently fingered the gift. The youth told her that there was only one spot where such extraordinary shells could be found. When he named the place, a certain bay several miles away, the teacher was left speechless. "Why . . . why, it's gorgeous . . wonderful, but you shouldn't have gone all that way to get a gift for me." His eyes brightening, the boy answered, "Long walk part of the gift!"[1]

2. A God Who Suffers With Us

But Isaiah's vision goes further than steasfast love. The prophet also speaks of a God Who Suffers With Us. He writes, "In all their affliction, God was afflicted . . ." The prophet dares to suggest that in all the Hebrew people have suffered over the centuries from slavery in Egypt to exile in Babylon, the Living God has suffered right beside them. Moreover, the God we meet in Jesus Christ is a God who voluntarily gave up all the privileges and powers of the Almighty to become a human being in our world — to feel what we feel, to suffer what we suffer — to be tempted just as we are tempted.

Can you visualize even for a moment the bridge God crossed from divinity to humanity? Can you visualize a God who has suffered physical torture, rejection, the abandonment of friends, betrayal, and even death itself? This is the God about whom Isaiah speaks whom you and I are privileged to know in the person of Jesus Christ.

Years ago I remember someone telling a modern parable of the Last Judgment. All the people on earth were gathered before Almighty God on a great plain, but they were an angry crowd. They mumbled and murmured about what right God had to judge their lives. There were black slaves who questioned how God could possibly understand the indignities and humiliation they had suffered at the hands of white oppressors. There were Jewish victims of the Holocaust who angrily protested God's ability to judge their lives without having lived through the horror of the gas chambers. On and on it went with the world's people questioning God's right to judge them until someone came up with an idea. Representatives from every group on earth would draw up a bill of particulars that God must fulfill before any judgment could take place. Here is what was included in that set of requirements for God:

Let God be born as a poor Jew.
Let God be rejected by the most important people of the time.

47

Let God's only friends be those who are held in contempt
   by the world.
Let God be betrayed by someone trusted.
Let God be indicted and convicted on false charges in
   a court.
Let God know torture, abandonment by friends, and the
   finality of death.

As this bill of particulars was read off to the assembled multitudes gathered on the plain, a great cheer went up. Then it grew strangely quiet as one by one the world's people began to realize that God had already in Jesus Christ suffered every single requirement on that list! The great hold of Jesus Christ on the hearts of people lies simply in the fact that God has already walked in our human shoes, sat where we must sit, and experienced every form of suffering we can ever endure. The God we worship this morning is a God who suffers with us, and that may well be the most comforting assurance that we can ever know in our times of suffering and pain.

3. A God Who Saves Us

Isaiah pictures a God of steadfast love who suffers with us in our afflictions. But his portrait of the living God becomes even more dramatic when he insists that God is the One Who Saves. Isaiah writes, "God became their Savior. In his love and his pity, he redeemed them; he lifted them up and carried them all the days of old." Time after time in Israel's history, God had saved the Hebrew people from destruction. It was God who saved them from the persecution of the Egyptians; it was God who parted the waters of the Red Sea to save that remnant from sure destruction; it was God who saved the people from the attacks of the other Canaanite tribes; it was God who saved the people when both the northern and southern kingdoms were destroyed; and it is this same God who comes in Jesus Christ as the Divine Physician to heal and to restore our human lives that are soiled and broken by our sinful disobedience.

48

Only a God who gave us the gift of life can restore us to life in all its eternal fullness. Only a God who has shared our brokenness and despair can so redeem us that we find wholeness and hope. Only a God of great mercy can cleanse us from our sin, and touch our lives in such a way that we begin living our days in at least part of the fullness and richness our Creator intended. There is an old poem titled, "The Touch Of The Master's Hand," that comes to mind at this time of year. In a simple and beautiful way, it describes the God we know in Jesus Christ as our Savior.

The Touch Of The Master's Hand
Myra Brooks Welch

'Twas battered and scarred, and the auctioneer
Thought it scarcely worth his while
To waste much time on the old violin,
But he held it up with a smile.

"What am I bidden, good folks," he cried,
"Who will start bidding for me?
A dollar, a dollar" — then "Two!" "Only two?
Two dollars and who'll make it three?"
"Going for three . . ." But no,
From the room, far back, a gray-haired man
Came forward and picked up the bow;
Then, wiping the dust from the old violin,
And tightening the loose strings,
He played a melody pure and sweet
As sweet as a caroling angel sings.

The music ceased, and the auctioneer,
With a voice that was quiet and low,
Said, "What am I bidden for the old violin?"
And he held it up with the bow.
"A thousand dollars, and who'll make it two?
Two thousand! And who'll make it three?
Three thousand, once, three thousand twice,
And going, going, gone!" said he.

49

The people cheered, but some of them cried,
"We do not quite understand
What changed its worth?" Swift came the reply:
"The touch of the Master's hand."

And many a man with life out of tune,
And battered and scarred with sin,
Is auctioned cheap to the thoughtless crowd,
Much like the old violin.
A "mess of pottage," a glass of wine;
A game — and he travels on.
He's "going" once and "going" twice,
He's "going" and "almost gone."

But the Master comes, and the foolish crowd
Never can quite understand
The worth of a soul, and the change that's wrought
By the touch of the Master's hand.[2]

As we finish another year and prepare to enter into a new one, many of our lives need that touch of the Master's hand. The God about whom Isaiah wrote so long ago and whom we meet in Jesus Christ is none other than the master architect of human life. God's touch can change lives that are out of tune, lives that are battered and scarred by years of sinful living. As we continue to celebrate this wondrous Christmas season, let this be a time when we draw close to God and discover again the God of steadfast love, the God who suffers with us, and the God who redeems us in amazing grace and mercy.

"So, What's New?"

"So, what's new?" he asked. It happens all the time. You meet someone on the street you have not seen for awhile. "What's new?" "Oh, nothing much, really. How 'bout with you?" That's the way a lot of conversations go, but I wonder what would happen if just once as a Christian I had the courage to respond: "I'll tell you what's new — it's the good news of what God has done for this world in Jesus Christ!" That would be a startling answer, but here at the beginning of a new year, that kind of bold announcement might be a refreshing change from the hackneyed, "Happy New Year," or the clever greeting someone gave me this past week: "Pastor, may all your troubles last as long as your New Year's resolutions!"

So what is new about what God has done for the world in the lives of the Hebrew people and supremely in Jesus Christ? The prophet Jeremiah — who incidentally, was not a bullfrog as the old song implies — announces in our text some of the new things that God has in mind for the people of Israel following the terrible experiences of exile and dispersion. In fact, in some of the most memorable and poignant words the Old Testament has to offer, Jeremiah lays out in very human terms the new age that God will inaugurate when Israel is restored and the Messiah reigns in power over this earth. Jeremiah suggests at least three dramatic changes that can take place right now if we will let God's Messiah, Jesus Christ, reign in our hearts in this new year.

1. A New Beginning

First is the promise of a new beginning. Jeremiah says, "The Lord has saved the people, the remnant of Israel. The Lord has ransomed Jacob and has redeemed him from hands too strong for him." Do you hear those key words? Jeremiah speaks of God saving us, ransoming us, redeeming us and that is precisely the new beginning God offers each of us in Jesus Christ! This is no vague injunction to "look on the brighter side of things in the new year." I chuckled over the little boy who signed up for Little League baseball. After the first day his father asked him how he made out. Billy replied: "The coach says I'm the best of the worst three!" That's a wonderful attitude, but the new beginning Jeremiah speaks of is something far more radical. It is nothing less than the opportunity to wipe the past slate clean, to start over again, to know one's life is cleansed by the forgiving grace of God in Jesus Christ.

Jim was a business executive who had been in and out of church for most of his life. Last year during Lent, Jim was invited to join a small group in his church that was committed to studying the Bible, praying and sharing together for six weeks. The six weeks were wonderful, but something very unexpected happened on the last evening together. The leader invited the members to share anything new in their lives as a result of their time together. Jim found himself saying, "I am forgiven" and he choked up. Tears began to flow down his cheeks. He repeated the words once more, "I know I am forgiven." Jim's life would never be the same again.

Diane had a similar experience in another Lenten group. For 15 years she had carried inside her soul the hurt of a divorce and the awful sense that she had failed herself, her family, her church and her God. Through the weeks together in the group, she put others to the test as if trying to prove that this forgiveness and grace everyone talked about could not possibly be for her. It was several weeks after the group ended that from deep inside Diane came a witness of the Holy Spirit, and she suddenly knew that God's forgiveness was for her! A radiant new person emerged from a 15-year-old cocoon.

The history of Christianity begins for every person at precisely this same starting point. Mary Magdalene, Martin Luther, you and I, we all start over when the awesome reality of God's forgiving grace enters our lives. This is why God's Son came into our world — to make possible in God's love a new beginning.

2. A New Belonging

But Jeremiah's vision of a new age includes not only a new beginning but a new belonging as well. "Behold, says the Lord, I will bring them from the north country, and gather them from the farthest parts of the earth. He who scattered Israel will gather him, and will keep him as a shepherd keeps his flock." George Gallup is continually discovering millions of Americans who think of themselves as "believers" but not "belongers." But there is no such possibility in the kingdom of God. God's plan from the very beginning was to make a united people who would reveal God's glory to the nations. Jesus brought people into a community of faith. Christians were never meant to be isolated individuals. We are bound together in Jesus by the Spirit to serve as witnesses to all the world that God's love overcomes all barriers.

How broken our lives are when we try to live them separately! How desperately we need to be bound together in love! How little we know of God's grace when we isolate ourselves or even hide from one another! I often recall the fellow who moved into a new town and decided to visit a number of churches. Some had great preaching. Others had beautiful buildings and fabulous youth and music programs. But one day he came into a little church a few minutes late. The people were praying a prayer together and the words of the prayer were: "We have done those things we ought not to have done, and we have left undone those things we ought to have done." When the prayer ended, the man turned to the person next to him and said, "Thank God. I think I have found my crowd at last!" But you see, that is God's design that we be knit together in a family of faith, a people who belong together in the common experience of God's grace in Jesus Christ.

Sometimes, however, we forget Jeremiah's vision of a whole people belonging to God and instead, we set limits on God's love and grace. I remember reading of a pastor who was trying to bring a young black man to a place where he would accept Christ as his savior. The young man listened and then told this story. When he had been a boy of 10 or 11, they had a revival in his town in the white church. The black boy and his mother went for several nights and sat in the back pew. Night after night the boy heard the stories about the love of Jesus. It excited him and thrilled him. Then the leader of the revival announced that everyone who believed in Jesus and wanted to be baptized, should be at the river at a certain time and should wear a white robe. The boy's mother made him a white robe and he went down the next day to the river. All the other people at the river were white, but that did not bother the boy because he knew he loved Jesus and Jesus loved him. They began baptizing men and women, boys and girls. All of them were baptized and then they left. All of them, that is, except this little black boy. They left him standing by the river alone.[1]

Jesus died because of prejudice like that, but he rose from the dead to demonstrate for all time that hatred and prejudice and every evil that keeps us apart can be conquered by the amazing and limitless love of God. We can experience a new belonging in this year if we let the Spirit of God draw us into the community of faith where it is possible to love others as God has loved us in Christ.

3. A New Being

Jeremiah's vision includes not only a new beginning and a new belonging, but the possibility of a whole new being. The prophet speaks of people "being radiant over the goodness of the Lord," and promises a life where God will turn "mourning into joy." Those words suggest a whole new life where love, justice, righteousness, peace, truth and purity become the hallmarks of everyday life.

Some years ago I saw a T-shirt that had a picture of an apple on the front with a bite taken out of it. Above the apple was written "Not Perfect." Below the apple were the words "Just Forgiven." Now that is clever, but I have some trouble with that message. There is no question about our being "Not Perfect." That's my story and your story! What bothers me is the phrase "Just Forgiven." We are not just forgiven! This is not a gospel about a ticket to heaven, but a gospel of transforming power for life right now! God intends those who make a new beginning in Christ who now belong to a new community, to look and act like new persons! We are not just forgiven so we can stay sinners. We are forgiven and renewed so that we can become the agents of God's reconciliation in this world. To put it another way, think of the familiar lines of the hymn "Amazing Grace." Why would God want to "save a wretch like me" just to leave me "a wretch!" We are a people who have been saved in order to serve, and that ought to show in our daily living.

Do you recall the old story of why the man fell out of bed? According to the story, he stayed too close to where he got in! Do you know why some people fall out of church and out of a vital relationship with Jesus Christ? The same answer, they stay around the edges of the gospel. They attend, they sing, they pray and they give, but they fail to make that inner surrender in their heart to the Living Christ that opens the way for us to become new beings — whole new people in Christ. We are like the woman who picked up a bottle of perfume at the store counter and tried it. The salesperson said,

"This perfume is called 'Surrender' and it is our hottest item. Would you like to try it?" The woman hesitated and then said, "It's nice, but do you have anything called 'Negotiate'?"

Unfortunately a lot of us want something less than a surrender of our lives to the Living Lord. But a new being and a truly new year in our lives become possible only when we put our lives into the hands of the master and let God reshape us into the likeness of Christ, and use us in bringing righteousness and redemption to the whole world.

In a hotel in Norway a little girl loved to play the piano. She knew one song, and every morning she would play that song much to the disgust of the guests. It did not seem to be a very pretty song and she did not play it very well. But one night a famous pianist stayed at that hotel. In the morning he was awakened by the little girl playing her song. He quickly threw on his robe and went downstairs to where the child was playing. He said to her, "I know that song. Will you let me play it along with you?" The little girl said, "Yes," and the pianist sat down at the keyboard and with the child on his lap, began playing that same melody. But this time it was so beautiful that everyone stopped to listen. The girl played along with the pianist but the music blended so well because the master player was in control. If we will give our lives to Christ, something of that new radiance and joy that Jeremiah foretold so long ago will help us become new beings in Christ.

So, what's new in this new year? In Jesus Christ you and I can have a new beginning, a new belonging, and a new being. That's good news! Why don't you share that good news the next time someone says to you, "What's new?"

Light For Our Darkness

The Feast of Christmas celebrates God's wondrous gift of Jesus Christ to be the Savior of the world. The Feast of Epiphany celebrates our human gifts to God, symbolized by those gifts given by the wise men to the Christ Child. More than any other characters in the Christmas story, the three wise men have been the subject of much good humor. Perhaps you recall the story of the little boy who was setting up a manger scene in the corner of his schoolroom. Puzzled for a moment, he called out to his teacher, "And where shall I put the three wise guys?"

The truth is we know very little about these ancient astrologers. We have assumed that there were three of them, because Matthew speaks of three different gifts being given to the Christ Child. We can only guess at the fact that they must have been persons of wealth because of the magnificence of their gifts. However, if we are to understand why the magi of old made that long journey to Bethlehem, we must go back to the prophecy of Isaiah.

When Isaiah wrote about caravans of camels bringing gold and frankincense, he was speaking of a time when the Jewish people would return to Jerusalem after their long exile in Babylon. The Persian emperor, Artaxerxes, was allowing Jerusalem to become one of his fortified cities. It was a time when gold, incense, lumber, stone and building materials would come from all parts of the Persian Empire. But for someone like Isaiah who looked at history with the eyes of faith, this was the end of the dark times for Israel, and the sign of new hope and blessing. The Lord God of Israel was breaking away the clouds of doom and the storms of despair, so that a new light of hope would come upon God's people.

When Matthew was writing many hundreds of years later, he remembered the prophecy of Isaiah about the light of God breaking forth in the midst of the earth's darkness. For him and for us, Jesus Christ is the brightest light God would ever send to this earth. So let's ask how the vision of Isaiah is fulfilled in the experience of the wise men. Here are some possibilities:

1. God's Guidance

One of the most significant facts about these ancient astrologers was their openness and willingness to follow God's guidance. Isaiah's opening words call the people of God to be open to God's leading: "Arise, shine; for your light has come, and the glory of the Lord has risen upon you." The magi knew that the star which they followed was no ordinary star. These three had apparently been searching the heavens for years for signs of something unique and significant occurring in their world. They were open to new wisdom and truth, and when they perceived a star brighter than any they had ever seen, they sensed in their hearts that this was a sign from God.

How do people receive guidance like that from God? How do you and I know when God is speaking? Clearly, people of faith must be looking for the signs of God's presence, and making full use of the spiritual disciplines they possess. Isn't it amazing that these magi from a foreign land are the first to see this great star in the heavens, while King Herod and his prophetic advisors do not even take a moment to gaze into the Judean heavens! Thomas Edison was right. Genius is 98 percent perspiration and two percent inspiration! The Living God still speaks to women and men whose eyes are open to the signs of God's presence in the world about them, and whose hearts are open and receptive as they read the scriptures and as they pray.

Do you recall the humorous story of the pastor who waited until Saturday night to prepare a message for Sunday? Halford Luccock describes this distraught man going to his bookshelves, taking down one book after another, and mumbling to himself, "Nothing to preach about here." Finally the preacher takes down the Bible. After thumbing through its pages frantically, he says in despair, "Nothing to preach about here, either!" The magi reminded us on this Epiphany that God's guiding light is seen by those who are searching diligently for it.

2. Going Forth In Faith

A second way in which Isaiah's prophecy comes alive in the experience of the magi is their willingness to go forth on their incredible journey of faith. Isaiah speaks of a time when "nations shall come to your light and kings to the brightness of your rising." Faith, by definition, involves us in a journey. That has to be a personal journey. Meaningful faith in the Living God cannot be found by proxy. That was Herod's mistake. He wanted the magi to go in his place and search for the child. Only then would he come and worship the newborn king. By contrast, the magi had to travel from a foreign land in search of wisdom and truth. They presumably could have sent out their servants on this long journey, but instead they made this a personal quest, and the result was an opportunity to worship the one who would be King of kings and Lord of lords.

This may well be the most important truth for us in the Epiphany story. A story of faith with Jesus Christ has to be a personal quest. It is not enough to know about Jesus Christ. One must encounter the wonder of God's grace for sinners, and then make a personal decision to receive Christ into our hearts as Lord. No one else can do that for you. Faith is not inherited like the family jewels, and yet hundreds of people have never made a personal faith commitment like that of the ancient wise men. I had an experience not long ago that I suspect is not unlike one many of us have. I was cleaning out a file of old college term papers. The one which struck a chord in me was a 16-page wonder on the "Contributions Of Pope Leo The Great" which I had written in one night for a course in Medieval History. It was outwardly impressive: I had two pages of footnotes, and a long bibliography of books I had barely scanned. The fact that I got a B on that paper was a triumph of generosity over good judgment on the part of my professor. But what caught my attention was the fact that I managed to tell the professor everything anyone had ever said about Pope Leo, but never once in 16 pages did I say a thing about what the study of that great Christian saint's life had meant to me.

In like manner, you and I can have a term paper relationship with Jesus Christ. We can know about Jesus, we can sing about Jesus, we can even use the name of Jesus when we pray, but our faith journey is not a personal one until like the magi of old, we involve ourselves, heart, mind and soul, in discovering what it means to know Christ personally.

3. Giving Generous Gifts

Yet a third place where the wise men light up the prophecy of Isaiah is in the bringing of generous gifts to the Christ. Isaiah pictures camels bringing costly gifts of gold and frankincense in celebration of Israel's return to the glory of Jerusalem. At Epiphany I almost always recall the cartoon which

60

showed the three wise men riding across the desert. One turns to the others and says, "Why didn't you guys tell me you were getting such expensive gifts?" They were expensive gifts as were the ones described by Isaiah, and they symbolize a response of the heart to God's wondrous gift of the light and love of Christ.

Material substance and how we use it has always been an indication of the true loyalty of the human heart. In a world where if you lined up the hungry and the homeless in a single file line, that line would stretch 25 times around the globe, it is amazing to consider how we use our material resources. UNICEF has calculated that 100 million children will die in the decades of the 1990s. At least half of those children could be saved by simple measures such as immunization and medication. The estimated cost is $2.5 billion. That is about the same amount the American cigarette companies spend on advertising each year, or that Soviet citizens spend in a month on vodka. How painfully those statistics speak of what is truly important in the human heart! Isaiah on the other hand saw the precious gifts of material wealth being used to restore the radiance and glory of God's people in Jerusalem, and the wise men present their gifts to the holy family as outward tokens of their devotion and love for God.

One can only think of Henry Van Dyke's famous story of *The Other Wise Man*. Artaban was a king who started out to join the other three in following the great light of the Bethlehem Star. But all along the way, he encountered people in such desperate human need, that he uses up all the treasures he had brought for the Christ Child. It took him more than 30 years to find Jesus, and when he does, Jesus is dying on a cross. Artaban says, "Three and 30 years have I looked for you, but I have never seen your face." And the voice of Jesus says, "Inasmuch as you did it unto one of the least of these, you did it unto me." Artaban's face became suddenly radiant. His quest was ended. His generous giving had brought him face to face with Jesus Christ.

4. Glory Of God Revealed

One final truth that Isaiah lights up for us in the Epiphany Story is the glory of God being revealed in the midst of the world's darkness. Wrote the prophet, "Darkness shall cover the earth, but the Lord will rise upon you and God's glory will be seen upon you." Many people like Herod and his court missed the coming of the Messiah, because they could not imagine the glory of God being revealed in a stable! J. B. Phillips reminded us many years ago in his little book, *Your God Is Too Small.* So many of us limit our glimpses of God's glory in everyday life because we simply do not expect the living God to break into our lives while we work in the office, sit in our classrooms, or do dishes at the kitchen sink. But the glory of God is still breaking into the world's darkness for all who look with the eyes of faith.

One of my favorite Christmas stories is about the man who hated Christmas. It was Christmas Eve, but in spite of his wife's pleas, he would not accompany her to church. The whole crazy idea of God becoming a human being made no sense to his logical mind. He stood watching the heavy snow from his picture window. He thought of the birds and wondered if they would find the seeds he had put out for them. It was snowing so hard that the seed holders were quickly covered. He turned on the backyard lights, but both the birds and the seed were lost in the swirling snow. Putting on his heavy coat, he went outside and opened his big barn door. Then he spread birdseed just inside the barn, hoping that the birds would see it. They did not! Still hoping to help these little starving creatures, the man tried desperately to shoo the little birds toward the light of his open barn, but they were too frightened. Here they were inches away from the food and water they desperately needed, and he was helpless. " If only I were a bird, I would show them the way to that life-giving food, " he thought to himself. Just then the church bells began to ring announcing Christmas morning. Suddenly the man understood why God's Son came to show us the way to life eternal. That is God's glorious light for our darkened world! Arise, shine, for your light has come!

Mission Possible

Almost all of us have seen the popular television program, "Mission Impossible." For many years the MI Task Force took on what seemed like an incredible assignment, and in less than an hour, they did the impossible! How wonderful it would be if carrying out the mission of Jesus Christ in this world were as easy.

The challenge to us in this season of Epiphany is the on-going proclamation that the "light shines in the darkness, and the darkness has not overcome it (John 1:5)." But in more ways than one, this is often the darkest time of the year. The familiar Christmas carols have been sung and now fade into pleasant memory. The family once gathered is now dispersed. The Christmas candle is now extinguished, and the earth once more spins in the shadows of bombs blasting, depression, drugs, broken resolutions and broken relationships. Even in Bethlehem where the star shone so brightly, there are cries for justice and the sounds of gunfire and death.

Perhaps, then, this is a good time for us to listen again to the Servant Song of Isaiah that describes the mission of God's Messiah. The prophet sees God's chosen one as a light given to the nations who will bring forth justice to the earth. Clearly, it was this vision of Isaiah that shaped our Lord's ministry

63

on this earth, and that same vision can shape our lives as we continue that same ministry in Christ's name. What, then, are the essential elements according to Isaiah of Mission Possible?

1. Ministry Of Justice

One vital element in Christ's mission on this earth is a ministry of justice. The prophet speaks again and again of "bringing forth justice," and "establishing justice on this earth." But what is justice? Like the words mercy and peace, justice is a key word in the scripture that is often misunderstood. I often think of the student who preached a first sermon in the seminary chapel. The instructor after a long pause said, "Your sermon today reminds me of the mercy and peace of God. Like God's mercy it seemed to endure forever, and like God's peace, it passed all human understanding!"

The dictionary defines justice as "the standards by which the benefits and penalties of living in society are distributed." But the followers of Jesus Christ have always wanted to go much further than that. Paul Tillich in his book, *Love, Power and Justice*, says that for a Christian, justice must be defined in terms of God's grace and forgiveness. Christianity has always tried to reduce the fundamental inequalities in the world; it has never accepted the premise that some human beings are more equal than other human beings. For a Christian, justice is violated whenever people are treated as if they were things. Throughout Jesus' ministry, we see our Lord challenging both individuals and the society whenever someone was being treated as less than a child of God.

There are always two vital aspects to a church's ministry: the pastoral and the prophetic. By pastoral, I mean the ministries our church conducts that include worship, the sacraments, counseling and teaching, visitation and prayer. The prophetic ministry on the other hand, consists of challenging the individual and society to reckon with both the judgment and mercy of God. This is the church's ministry that addresses us in the

64

crucible of daily life, bridging suburbs and slums, affluence and poverty, war and peace, comfort and challenge.

For many congregations, the pastoral ministry gets the lion's share of the time and energy of both laity and clergy. Such ministries are also much safer. The prophetic ministry on the other hand, is often lonely and dangerous. But as Isaiah reminds us, and Jesus' life confirms, the prophetic ministry is central, not marginal, in the biblical tradition. The prophets saw sickness, identified it, and pointed beyond it to the divine cure. They were not people eager to be antagonistic or contentious, or people who found delight in delivering salvos against the existing order. But the prophets were people of God who were filled with courage and zeal and who were willing to risk whatever it cost to condemn injustice in any form.

Listen to the blunt words of the prophet Amos: "I hate, I despise your feasts, and I take no delight in your solemn assemblies . . . but let justice roll down like waters and righteousness like an everflowing stream." That imagery has always reminded me of the turbulent Colorado River tumbling and rushing its way through the Grand Canyon. So justice is meant to be a mighty stream, no mere trickle! It relates directly to God's basic concern for life, for the health and wholeness of every human being. Now this is no philosophical abstraction we debate. This is nothing less than the love of Christ in action. Justice deals with the hurt and wrong against individuals and groups, not simply in the past, but here and now.

I believe that God is calling the church in our time to recover this all important prophetic aspect to our ministry. God desires sons and daughters who will become co-workers with Christ in the bringing forth of justice. For a long time in this country, we have seen a mood of inwardness and self concern. Some of this is healthy, but a lot of it is neurotic. We can so easily become distracted with our own growth that we never see or feel the hurt, pain and evil our busyness permits to go unchecked in society. We can so easily get wrapped up in our tight little world of work, home, school and leisure that we do not even see the times and places all around us when human beings are being treated as if they were things.

I am reminded of the mother taking her little boy for a walk. They came to a nudist camp surrounded by a high board fence. When the child peeped through a small hole in the fence, the mother asked, "What do you see?" The boy responded, "A lot of people." "Are they men or women?" inquired the mother. "I don't know," said the boy, "nobody's got any clothes on!" Most of us have more information than we care to act upon. We plead ignorance or heavy schedules, but the truth is our indifference is what allows injustice to continue on this earth.

But Isaiah reminds us that the church has a mandate from God to meddle in life. Justice is God's business and every follower of the Living Christ is called to this dangerous and often costly ministry. For some Christians, the ministry of justice has meant the loss of friendships. For others it has meant imprisonment and even death. During World War II, the small town of Le Chambon in Southern France gave the world a remarkable example of Christian justice at work. Quietly, in full view of the Vichy government, and a nearby division of Nazi storm troopers, the villagers organized to save thousands of Jewish children and adults from certain death in the gas chambers. But these brave Christians protested when anyone praised them. "How can you call us 'good'? We are simply doing what had to be done. Who else could help those poor people? We happened to be there and we knew that this is what God wanted us to do."

Sister Miriam Therese Winter has written a song that calls us all to recapture the ministry of justice. It is titled, *Take The Time.*

> *Take the time to sing a song*
> *for all those people who don't belong:*
> *the women wasted by defeat,*
> *the men condemned to walk the street,*
> *the down and out we'll never meet.*
>
> *Take the time to hear the plea*
> *of every desperate refugee:*

the millions who have had to flee
their lands, their loves, their liberty,
who turn in hope to you and me.

Take the time to take a stand
for peace and justice in every land.
Where power causes deep unrest,
come, take the part of the oppressed,
and then, says God, you will be blessed.[1]

2. The Ministry Of Light

Isaiah speaks of another element in God's mission possible for this world, and that is the ministry of light. Isaiah says that the Servant will be "a light to the nations to open the eyes that are blind." Jesus spoke of himself as the Light of the World, and then in the Sermon on the Mount, our Lord said that "you are the light of the world." Light is essential to life, isn't it? If you have ever tried to pick your way through the woods at night without a flashlight, then you know the value of light. Businesses often leave lights on at night because the FBI says that 75 percent of all crimes are done in the dark. It was Goethe as he was dying who cried out, "Light! More light!" The world has often echoed that same cry, and that is why God sent Jesus Christ to lead us out of darkness into the marvelous light of God.

If you think about it, light is a very helpful image when it comes to understanding our place in Christ's mission. Light is often a way of expressing what it means to come to a new understanding of something. We suddenly exclaim, "At last I see the light." Sometimes we parents would prefer it if our children remained in the dark a little longer. I think of that poor mother who was suddenly confronted with the inevitable question, "Where do babies come from?" She paused, wishing that her husband were home to answer their little son. In a moment of inspiration she said, "Well, the Bible says we are all made from dust . . . dust thou art unto dust returneth."

67

The little boy seemed satisfied until he went up to his room and looked under his bed. "Mommy, come quick," he shouted. "There are lots of babies under my bed and I can't tell if they are coming or going!"

Not all new understanding in the form of light is easy to grasp, but in the coming of Jesus Christ, the world was given a whole new understanding of the love and mercy of God. It was as if a bright light was suddenly turned on in the world. Not only was the dust and dirt in our lives exposed, but in Christ, the world discovered how far God was willing to go to reconcile us and redeem us. Belmont Abbey College in North Carolina sits on property that was once a large southern plantation. The land was given to the Catholic Church, and the abbey and college were built upon it. In a far back corner of the property, the monks found a huge granite stone, upon which men, women and children stood little more than a century ago to be sold as slaves. The monks took the stone and hollowed a little bowl in the top. Then they carried it into the abbey's chapel where to this day, it serves as a baptismal font. The engraving on it reads: "Upon this rock, men were once sold into slavery. Now upon this rock, through the waters of baptism, people become free children of God." That's a wonderful symbol of the new light that Jesus Christ has brought into our world in terms of a whole new understanding of God.

We are privileged to be light-bearers for Jesus Christ, but as we take our places beside the Living Lord in bringing light to our darkened world, let us never forget that "the light shines in the darkness, and the darkness will never overcome it."

Improving Your Serve

Charles Swindoll in his popular book, *Improving Your Serve*, tells of how he was at first haunted and then convicted by the Bible's insistence that Jesus came not to be served, but to serve and to give his life a ransom for many (Mark 10:45)." The more he studied what the Bible says about servanthood, the more convinced Swindoll became that our task in this world, like that of Jesus, is not to be served, not to grab the spotlight, and not to become successful or famous or powerful or idolized. Our calling is to be authentic servants who genuinely give of themselves without concern over who gets the glory.

For many of us, that term servant may conjure up an image somewhere between an African slave named Kunta Kinte straight out of *Roots*, and those thousands of migrant workers who, at harvest time, populate the farmlands and orchards of America. In my mind is a rather pathetic person, bent over, crushed in spirit, lacking in self esteem, soiled, wrinked and weary. And my first response is "Who, me, a servant? You gotta be kidding!"

If that is the kind of mental picture you have of servanthood, then the prophet Isaiah has some good news for you. In our text for this day, Isaiah paints a kind of word portrait of the Lord's servant. Now biblical scholars will continue to ask, "Who is meant by the servant in these verses? Is Isaiah speaking of himself, of Israel, or of a future messianic figure?" We can leave that debate to the scholars, because the Christian tradition has always read these servant songs in the light of Jesus and his ministry. Clearly, Isaiah's vision of the servant gave form and substance to Jesus' ministry, and to our calling to be the servants of Christ in the world today. So, let's let Isaiah introduce us to authentic servanthood.

1. God's Call To Be A Servant

Isaiah makes this calling of God intense and personal. "The Lord called me from the womb, from the body of my mother he named my name." God has called the servant and has given the servant a name before that person was ever born! Now recall that for the Hebrews, the name not only identified the person, but shaped the reality of the person's character. The prophet uses this vivid language to remind us that God's grace precedes any possible human merit or ability.

I recall a line from some unknown poet that goes, "How odd of God to choose the Jews." Israel as a people always had trouble understanding what it meant to be called to be a servant people. But election by God both for Israel and for us has nothing to do with our human merit, nor with being a privileged people. From the beginning God has chosen people for the sake of humankind. We are chosen, set apart, elected, not because of any worth on our part, but by God's grace, to call all the ends of the earth to salvation. How often, in our struggles to proclaim our self-importance, do we forget that it is the living God who calls us to be servants!

A senator, a clergyman and a Boy Scout were passengers in a small plane that developed engine trouble. "We'll have to bail out," the pilot announced. "Unfortunately, there are only three parachutes. I have a wife and seven small children.

70

My family needs me. I'm taking one of the parachutes." And he jumped. "I'm the smartest politician in the world," said the senator. "The country needs me. I'm taking one of the parachutes." And he jumped. "I've had a good life," said to the clergyman to the Boy Scout," and yours is still ahead of you. You take the last parachute." "Don't need to," shrugged the youth. "There are two parachutes left. The smartest politician in the world jumped with my knapsack!"

Servants are people of God to serve and to give. God wants to build into our lives the same serving and giving qualities that characterized the earthly life and ministry of our Lord. To me, it is always inspiring when someone in the public spotlight remembers this basic call of God to be a servant. Many of you will recall the name of Colonel James B. Irwin who was a part of the team of astronauts who made the successful moon walk. When Irwin returned, he spoke of the thrill connected with leaving this planet and seeing it shrink in size. He mentioned watching earthrise one day, and thinking how privileged he was to be a part of this unique crew. And then, as they were en route back to earth, he began to realize that the experience he had shared with his crew in space would make them overnight international celebrities. It was then that James Irwin, a person of deep faith in God, made a decision. In his own words, he said: "As I was returning to earth, I realized that I was a servant, not a celebrity. So I am here as God's servant on planet Earth to share what I have experienced that others might know the glory of God."[1]

That is still our calling from God — to be servants and not celebrities. Caught up in the fast lane of 20th century life, making mad dashes through airports, meeting deadlines, coping with the stress of meeting other people's demands and our own high expectations, it is very easy to lose sight of our primary calling as Christians. But God's plan from the very beginning has been to use human instruments for the redemption of the world. That is God's call since we were formed in our mother's womb — to be servants of the Living God.

71

2. God's Preparation Of The Servant

Isaiah's portrait of God's servant continues with a description of how the servant is prepared for a universal task. Wrote Isaiah, "He made my mouth like a sharp sword . . . he made me a polished arrow and in his quiver, he hid me away." The prophet's imagery suggests that God prepares servants with a sharpness that will penetrate the resistance of those in the sixth century B.C. or those in the 20th century A.D. who harden their hearts to the message of grace and salvation.

It is as if the piercing quality of the servant's message must break through the hardness of custom and conventionality which enamels peoples' minds and consciences.

Ours is a tough, rugged, wicked world. Aggression, rebellion, violence, cutthroat competition and retaliation abound, not just on an international level, but in our personal lives as well. According to a study done at the University of Rhode Island, the American home is the most dangerous place to be outside of riots and war. No less than 30 percent of all American couples experience some form of domestic violence in their lifetimes! Somewhere up to 15 million women are battered in our nation each year! The heart of humankind can be very hard. A tramp discovered that when one day he was looking for a handout in a picturesque old English village. Hungry almost to the point of fainting, he stopped by a pub bearing the classic name, "Inn of Saint George And The Dragon." "Please, ma'am, could you spare me a bit to eat?" he asked. The woman who answered his knock on the kitchen door took one look at him and said, "A bite to eat for a sorry, no good bum, a foul smelling beggar like you — No!" She slammed the door. Halfway down the lane the tramp stopped, turned around, and eyed the words "Saint George And the Dragon." He went back and knocked again on the kitchen door. "Now what do you want?" the woman asked angrily. "Well, ma'am, if Saint George is in, may I speak with him this time?"

That's the kind of resistance God's servant can expect to encounter, but the Spirit of God will, according to Isaiah, glorify the servant and use the servant's message to be "a light to the nations."

3. God's Universal Task For The Servant

But now, as Isaiah completes the portrait of God's servant, the prophet focuses on the universal task. "I will give you as a light to the nations, that my salvation may reach to the end of the earth." The imagery of light is very suggestive in understanding the servant's task. Light is silent. There's no noise, no big splash, no banners — light simply shines. It's like a single lighthouse on a rugged shoreline. All it does is shine forth its beacon as it turns.

Moreover, light attracts attention. You don't have to ask people to look when you turn a light on in a dark room. It happens automatically. If you are a Christian on an athletic team filled with non-Christians, you are the light in the darkness. If you are a Christian family in a non-Christian neighborhood, you are the light in that darkness. The same is true if you are the only Christian nurse on your floor, or professional in your firm, or student in your school. You are a light in darkness — a servant of God who is being watched, who gives off a very different message with hardly a word being said. At first, others may hate the light, but they cannot help being attracted by it.

Now the ancient Hebrews understood the importance of being a light, but they always had trouble with the idea that their light was to shine on more than just the house of Jacob. How easy it is in any age for a nation to think of itself as God's favorite! We quickly condemn the narrow focus of these ancient Hebrews or the British or the Germans in the modern era, but how quickly we Americans forget our 19th century policy of Manifest Destiny. God had given America great natural resources and we Americans can believe that our mission was to bring civilization to benighted nations, even if it meant conquering them for their own good.

73

Nowadays we are somewhat chastened and more realistic. We no longer regard ourselves as the civilizers of the world.

Instead there are many voices suggesting that, rich though we are, we have no responsibility for sharing with the hungry nations of the world if that means lowering our own standard of living. Paul Scherer suggests that we modern Americans are like the crew on a ship stocked with provisions to be carried to a sick and starving community. On the way the crew members forget the purpose of the voyage; they eat the bread and drink all the wine themselves. Maybe that sounds grotesque, but it is no more grotesque than nations as well as individuals, rich folk, cultured folk, church folk, sitting in the midst of plenty and consuming it, while all around us are the cries of God's other hungry, needy children.

The task of the servant in our world today is to be a giver. Let me encourage you, in spite of the high cost of giving and the small number of servant models you may see around you, to determine to be different. We are never more Godlike than when we give. Shortly after World War II, Europe began picking up the pieces. Perhaps the saddest sight of all was that of the little orphaned children starving on the streets of war-torn cities.

Early one morning an American soldier spotted a little lad with his nose pressed against the window of a pastry shop. Inside the baker was kneading dough for a fresh batch of doughnuts. The hungry boy stared in silence. His eyes glued to the glass as he watched those mouth-watering morsels being pulled from the oven, piping hot. The soldier's heart went out to the nameless orphan. Hurrying inside he quickly purchased a dozen hot doughnuts and took them outside to the hungry boy. "Would you like these doughnuts?" he asked. As he turned to walk away, the soldier felt a tug on his coat. He looked back and heard the child say, "Mister, are you God?" We are never more like God than when we give. The glory of being God's servant is the opportunity to do what God did in Jesus Christ our Lord. "For God so loved the world, that he gave . . . ."

74

Rejoice In The Lord

After a service of ordination to the Christian ministry, a sad-faced woman came up to the newly-ordained pastor and said, "It's a grand thing you are doing as a young man — giving up the joys of life to serve the Lord." That woman's attitude reflects a commonly held belief that to be serious about our faith means that we expect all joy to be taken out of living. For many, Christianity appears to be a depressing faith, with unwelcome disciplines, that cramps our lifestyle and crushes our spirits.

In a recent Doonesbury cartoon, an officer is standing by the bedside of a Navy sailor who is in sick bay aboard a cruiser. The officer says, "We've got you scheduled for surgery at four bells tomorrow! Your surgeon will be Commander Torres." As he leaves the officer says, "Well, take care, sport. I'll see you tonight during rounds." The sailor is puzzled and says to the officer, "What exactly do you do here?" The officer replies, "I'm ship's morale officer." And wide-eyed, the sailor says, "You mean, a . . . a chaplain?" And the officer replies, "No. No. I really do cheer people up!"

How sad that this word joy which Isaiah uses so many times in our text for today is so often thought to be the very opposite of faith! What a commentary that is on we Christians who seem to be saints with sour faces — people who talk about rejoicing before the Lord but who give little evidence of that joy in our living. When you turn to the pages of the Bible, you find that word joy or its variants being used more than 350 times in the scriptures. Isaiah speaks here of a new beginning in the history of Israel. The prophet forsees a time of light and peace after the terrible suffering Isaiah has endured in the long and oppressive reign of Tiglath-Pileser.

And when you turn to the New Testament, you find the story of Jesus beginning with the angelic announcement, "Behold, I bring you good tidings of great joy which shall be to all people." Jesus of Nazareth in his manhood was a joyful person. He took delight in the world about him. He found pleasure in all kinds of people, saints and scoundrels, children and foreigners, scholars and shepherds. Even on the night of his death, Jesus promised those who followed him the gift of joy, and encouraged them all to be of good cheer. When we look at those early Christians described in the Acts of the Apostles, it is their contagious joy which attracts so many to Christ. Clearly, our faith summons people not to a gloomy funeral, but to an exciting festival of life both now and in eternity.

What, then, is the joy that Isaiah says will come upon the people? Often we identify joy as being the same as happiness, and use those two words interchangeably. But happiness is something that occurs on an almost purely human level. In many cases, we can control our own happiness. Charles Schulz, the creator of "Peanuts," says that "Happiness is a warm puppy." My father used to say that "Happiness is simply having three square meals on the table every day." When I was a boy growing up, owning a Jackie Robinson baseball card meant you were the happiest kid in the class. To a teenage girl, happiness is being pursued by three guys at once. To a golfer, happiness is sinking a 25-foot putt. These things all bring pleasure to our lives and as long as we have them, they provide a contentment in our living.

But joy is something much deeper and much more lasting. Unlike happiness, we are not responsible for it. It comes into our lives as the gift of God. Joy is not like the superficial transient gaiety of a New Year's Eve party with its gray unpleasant consequences the morning after. Rather, joy breaks into our lives often in the most unexpected ways. It can be in a moment when love is expressed, when we are suddenly caught up in the unbelievable beauty of our world, or when that which is lost is found. There is the joy that comes in being forgiven when we have been wrong, the joy of being together when we have been separated, and the joy that one feels lingering in the heart, even when tears run down our cheeks.

You see, the joy of which Isaiah speaks is a gift of God. It is like a light shining in the darkness. It is not something we accomplish or achieve, or fashion, or even earn. We find joy as we find a treasure by surprise, or we are found by it as the wind finds the sail of our boat. As Teilhard de Chardin has said, "Joy is the most infallible sign of the presence of God." This remarkable joy has given the people of God in every age a zest and radiance in their living that goes far beyond just being "happy." I will never forget a sermon preached by the great church historian, Roland Bainton, shortly after his wife died. His text was Habakkuk 3:17:

> *"Though the fig tree does not blossom,*
> *nor fruit be on the vines . . .*
> *Yet, I will rejoice in the Lord.*
> *I will joy in the God of my salvation."*

For Dr. Bainton, and a host of God's people in every age, not even death can take away God's incredible gift of joy. That is clearly the same joy that the prophet Isaiah found in God at a time when there was little apparent joy among his people. Isaiah, in words that we have come to cherish, gives us three significant things about God in which we can rejoice.

1. Rejoice That God Lives

For one thing, we can rejoice that God lives. People in Isaiah's time felt that they had been living in total darkness.

77

Suffering and oppression had dominated their lives. But Isaiah says to them and to us who live in an age of pessimism, "The people who walked in darkness have seen a great light; those who dwelt in a land of deep darkness, on them has light shined." That was Isaiah's poetic way of affirming that God is very much alive and at work in the world. It is so easy for us to forget that in the kind of world that lives each day in the shadow of nuclear, chemical or biological warfare. If our human greed and selfishness don't destroy us, the population explosion and our pollution of the earth surely will. We know what it is to walk in darkness, and that is why we need to hear Isaiah's reminder that God lives.

On the night of May 5, 1863, a public meeting was held in Washington, and Frederick Douglass, the former slave, the great abolitionist orator was speaking. Then, somebody came in the back and whispered to those seated at the rear of the room, the shattering news that the Union Army had been defeated at Chancellorsville — 22,000 men either killed or wounded. Douglass stopped talking, for the audience rustled restlessly as the word spread up the aisles. Finally, someone handed Douglass a note with the message about the defeat. He read it, bowed his head in despair, and didn't know how he could go on. A murmuring panic began to descend over the auditorium until an old black woman in the balcony stood up, and called down to the stage, saying, "Frederick Douglass, God is not dead!"

No one can understand the real meaning of joy so long as we think of the universe as simply an accident, and our lives as sound and fury signifying nothing. But a person in Christ can rejoice even in the fiercest storm that our God lives, and that God will send the light we need in our darkness.

2. Rejoice That God Cares

But Isaiah holds out to his distraught people not only the knowledge that God lives, but the even more important truth that God cares. The prophet speaks of a time when "God will make glorious the way of the sea, the land beyond the Jordan, Galilee of the nations." Israel felt like a forgotten people. If God still existed, then God must be asleep, or at best, busy with other things. Like us, those ancient people knew the answer to the old catechism question, "What is the chief end of man?" "The chief end of man is to glorify God and enjoy him forever." But the way they were living, it seemed as if their chief end was to irritate God and annoy him forever!

Isaiah, however, believed in a God who cares, and who never stops caring even when we turn our backs on God. In ancient Rome, sensitive and cultured people for years had protested in vain the butcheries that took place in the arena. The bloody contests continued until one day, a Christian monk by the name of Telemachius leapt into the ring, and pushing himself between two gladiators, cried out, "In the name of Jesus Christ, stop!" A sword flashed, and the defenseless man fell to the ground. But it must have been the gesture the world was waiting for, because from that day onward, there were no more slaughters for the sake of sport in the city of Rome.

Perhaps this incident is something like what happened in Jesus Christ. The God we believe in is not One who sits passively on some cosmic grandstand, a detached spectator who looks on the suffering of human beings unmoved and uncaring. In Jesus Christ, God came into the arena of our struggles and agonies. It is because God has always been involved in the midst of life that we are called to get involved; it is because God cares so much, even to the point of death on a cross, that we must caringly minister to all for whom Christ died.

3. Rejoice That God's Plan Is Invincible

Finally, we can rejoice according to Isaiah in the assurance that God's plan is invincible. "The rod of the oppressor will be broken as on the day of Midian." A little more than 100 years ago, two faithful native friends entered David

79

Livingstone's tiny hut near the shore of Lake Tanganyika in Africa, and found that great missionary on his knees by his cot in the same position in death as he was frequently in life. They buried his heart in Africa, but carried his body 900 miles to the coast, so that eventually it could be laid to rest in Westminster Abbey. Evidently, Livingstone must have known the end was near. Only the day before, he had written these words in his journal:

> "I am a missionary, heart and soul. God had just one Son, and he, too, was a missionary. I have tried to be an imitation of him, though, I fear, a poor one. Looking back, I see few results for my labors, but God called me here, and I place no value on anything I have done except in relation to his kingdom which he is building and in which I am thankful to have been an apprentice. One day, Africa will belong to God's kingdom."[1]

It now appears that before the end of the 20th century, Africa will lead the world in its commitment to Jesus Christ. In a very real sense, every Christian is called to be a Livingstone. It does not matter what happens to us as long as the eternal work of God goes on. Our own failures and successes become minor, as long as the plan of God is undefeated. We rejoice that through life, there runs a purpose which decrees that every Calvary has its Easter, and every winter its resurgent spring. We rejoice that this corruptible will be put on incorruption, and that this mortal will put on immortality.

Isaiah was right: "The people who walked in darkness have seen a great light." Rejoice that God lives, that God cares, and that God's plan is invincible. Rejoice in the Lord!

The Bottom Line

One of the most common phrases heard in the marketplace today is "the bottom line." It makes no difference if you are buying a car, or a new house, a new wardrobe or planning a vacation. Whatever it is, we want to know how much will it cost. What's the bottom line?

There is a story going the rounds about a self-employed painter who had come on hard times. There was very little work in his area, so when he was asked to bid on the painting of a local church, he figured a little too closely to the bottom line. He got the job, but he soon realized that his bid was so low, he could not even make expenses. Feeling desperate, he decided to water down the paint. As the job was nearly finished, the sky grew dark, and it was not long before a raging thunderstorm washed the fresh paint completely off the church!

"It must be an act of God," he thought. He got down and looking up to heaven, he prayed, "O God, I'm sorry. How can I make this right?" A big, deep voice from heaven said, "My son, repaint and thin no more!"

Now you are probably saying that is not only bottom line thinking — that's bottom of the barrel! But let me raise an important question. Is there a bottom line in our religion? Is there something so basic, so fundamental, that we can say with

81

confidence, "This is the bottom line in our walk of faith." Long ago the prophet Micah asked a similar kind of question: "What does the Lord want from me?" Thinking of the religious heritage of his people, Micah wondered if burnt offerings were the thing God most wanted. Then he asks if God would be happier if we gave up one of our own children.

Suddenly there seems to break on the consciousness of this prophet the wonderful truth that what God most wants is not something but rather me! "What does the Lord require of you?" And then comes the surprising answer, "To do justice, and to love kindness, and to walk humbly with your God." All along Micah had assumed that the bottom line in religion was something that God wanted. But then, with the eyes of faith, he realizes what God most wants in response to what God has done is the commitment of our human hearts. Micah's familiar words provide a framework for how the people of God in every age are to live.

1. To Do Justice

The first aspect in bottom line religion emphasizes the social dimension: to do justice. Now you will notice that justice is something one does. To do justice means to work for the establishment of equity for all people, especially those who are powerless. Throughout this little book, Micah has provided many examples of the failure to do justice. He mentions how the powerful oppress the powerless, how laborers are exploited and courts are corrupted.

Sometimes when we hear the prophets call for doing justice, we can miss places in our contemporary lives where justice is needed. I have often appreciated a modern writer who paraphrases the familiar words of the prophet Amos: "Going to church on Sunday is no good unless your religion makes you honest on Monday. The money you put in the offering plate is money I do not want if it comes from ill-gotten gain. The anthems you sing make me sick, unless your living is in harmony with the Ten Commandments. If the person who raises the tune at Sunday school also raises the roof at home, if the person who offers long prayers in worship is also the person who makes the lives of employees miserable the rest of the week, then I despise your covered dish suppers and I take no delight in your dignified services of worship. But let civil rights roll down like waters and righteousness like an ever flowing stream.''[1]

That call to do justice often makes a lot of Christians uncomfortable in our time. Sometimes it is easier to say that what happens in the society, in politics, in business, or even in our homes is not the concern of the church. Our business, according to some, is to save souls and help needy individuals. Now that is certainly a part of our responsibility, but Jesus makes it very clear that our corporate response to the evil in this world must be just as important. It is a part of our service to God to help provide food and clothing to those in need, but is it not also our task to work to prevent the conditions that make human beings become refugees? It is certainly our task to comfort the family of a soldier killed on the battlefield, but is it not also our task to work for a just and lasting peace in the world? It is our task to comfort someone who has been a victim of violence, but is it not also our task to work to eliminate the causes of senseless violence in our homes and on our streets?

To do justice, then, involves us both as individuals and as a corporate body in bearing witness to the love of Jesus Christ for all persons. Recently I heard of a church that became quite concerned over a corporation in their community that was practicing dishonesty and deception in the production and marketing of a certain product. The officers of the church met and debated what should be done. Some people wanted to start a protest movement in that town. Others suggested an article in the paper condemning the corporation, while others favored a delegation going to the next stockholders' meeting. Instead, the officers prayed, asking God to make clear what their response should be.

Suddenly, someone remembered that two officers of the corporation attended that church. The officers as a body called on these two executives who were totally unaware of the enormity of the problem, and within two weeks of their visit, the offending product was withdrawn from the market! This is something of what it means in our time to do justice — to bring the Lordship of Jesus Christ into every area of our lives. To do justice is the first aspect of bottom line religion.

2. To Love Kindness

The second aspect of bottom line religion moves us from the social dimension to the personal: To love kindness. The word used by Micah means love with a strong element of loyalty, such as that between two dear friends. This is a kind of love that never quits. It is something radically different from the sentimental stuff of television soap operas. This is nothing less than a call to love others in the same incredible way that God has loved us in Jesus Christ. In our own human strength, such loving is impossible, but when we allow the Spirit of God to rule in our hearts, sometimes we are able to love even those who hurt us deeply.

Some years ago the noted columnist Bob Considine wrote a story titled, "Could You Have Loved This Much?" It was the true story of Edith Taylor, who for many years lived happily with her husband, Karl, in Waltham, Massachusetts. Then the government sent Karl to Okinawa on business. Edith stayed behind because of her job. Karl's letters became less and less frequent, and then one day he wrote to Edith saying that he had obtained a divorce in Mexico so that he could marry his Japanese servant girl, Aiko. Edith's life was shattered! She and Karl had been married 23 years. She still loved Karl and could not stop loving him. She accepted his decision, asking only that he write to her occasionally about his life.

It was in this way that Edith learned of the two daughters born to Karl and Aiko. Then came the dreadful news that

84

Karl was dying of lung cancer. Suddenly, Edith knew that her last gift to the man she loved was to send for that young Japanese wife and her two daughters, and offer them a place to live here in America. She prayed for many days, and when the news came of Karl's death, she sent for Aiko and her daughters. On a never to be forgotten day, Edith watched a frightened, pale, young woman and her daughters step off the airplane. There was a moment of hesitation, and then, both women rushed forward in a warm embrace of love.

Could you love that much? No human being in their own strength can show that sort of loving kindness, but with the help of God's Spirit, incredible things can happen! A love that never quits is the second aspect in bottom line religion.

3. To Walk With God

The third aspect in the sort of life God wants from us brings us to the spiritual or theological dimension: To walk humbly with God. Now the key word here is "walk." It suggests that the whole orientation of life centers in a daily walk of faith with the Lord. This call to walk is similar to Jesus' invitation to the disciples, "Follow me." Jesus seldom asks us "to believe," but rather to "come after me." One who so walks with God will not be exempt from the dark places of life, but that person lives each day in the assurance that he or she will never walk alone!

It is here that Micah's words really come alive for me in describing the kind of God with whom we walk each day. All that Micah has said about justice and about love helps us to grasp something of the greatness of this God we know in Jesus Christ. Dr. Martin Luther King, Jr. once wrote these meaningful words: "The greatness of God lies in the fact that God is both tough-minded and tenderhearted. God has qualities both of austerity and of gentleness. The Bible expresses God's tough-mindedness in his justice, and God's tenderness in his love and grace. God has two outstretched arms. One is strong enough to surround us with justice, and one is gentle enough to embrace us with grace. I am thankful we worship a God who is both tough-minded and tenderhearted. If God were only tough-minded, God would be a cold, passionless despot sitting in some far-off heaven. But if God were only tenderhearted, he would be too soft and sentimental to function when things go wrong. Thank the Lord for a God who is tough-minded enough to transcend the world, and yet, tenderhearted enough to live in it!''[2]

What's the bottom line in religion? The bottom line in terms of what God expects is to do justice, to love kindness and to walk humbly with a God who is both tough-minded and tenderhearted enough to be our Lord and our Savior.

Religion's Built-in Hazard

A Japanese legend says a pious Buddhist monk died and went to heaven. He was taken on a sightseeing tour and gazed in wonder at the lovely mansions built of marble and gold and precious stones. It was all so beautiful, exactly as he pictured it, until he came to a large room that looked like a merchant's shop. Lining the walls were shelves on which were piled and labeled what looked like dried mushrooms. On closer examination, he saw they were actually human ears. His guide explained that these were the ears of people who on earth went diligently to the temple, listened with pleasure to the teaching of the gods, yet, did nothing about what they heard. After death, they themselves went elsewhere, but only their ears made it to heaven.

We may smile at such a story, but the painful truth is that church people seem at times to be mostly ears — people who easily substitute hearing for doing. Religion has always had a built-in hazard. Believers are tempted to be good only for the show of it. The Greek word from which we derive our English term "hypocrite" literally means actor. And in every age, the great temptation of religious people is to go through the motions of piety without letting their faith permeate every aspect of their daily lives. I always marvel how just before

87

election, our public officials are careful to mention God in their speeches, and to be photographed going to their church or synagogue. We Americans would still like to believe that our public officials are pious men and women who acknowledge the rule of God.

Of course, many of our elected officials are people of genuine faith, but many others in spite of their public displays of piety, have turned out to be hypocrites, people who say one thing with their lips, and another with their lives. I often recall the story of the little boy who simply refused to go to Sunday school one week. His mother, trying desperately to encourage him, said, "Son, your father always went to Sunday school as a boy." The little boy looked at her with knowing eyes and said, "That's what I mean, Mom; it won't do me any good either!"

That's the painful truth about us all, and it was no different in the time of the prophet Isaiah. In fact people often made a great show of praying, almsgiving and fasting. Then, as now, it was easy to substitute a great public display of piety for concrete deeds of justice and compassion. People in Isaiah's time and even in the days of our Lord's earthly life would make a great spectacle of praying in the streets. In the synagogues of Jesus' time, announcements were made of gifts to the poor, and very large gifts were signaled by the blast of a trumpet. Those who fasted cultivated a lean and famished look, that others would know the full extent of their self-deprivation.

It must have been this insistence on winning public recognition for one's piety through fasting that really upset Isaiah. Looking about him at the needs of the homeless, the hungry and the oppressed, Isaiah could no longer keep still. The self-indulgent displays of sackcloth and ashes, he declares, are not acceptable to God! The only true way to observe a fast is by liberating the oppressed, sharing your bread with the hungry, and opening your own house to the homeless!

Now all this talk of fasting sounds almost ridiculous to our modern ears. In a culture where the landscape is dotted with shrines to the golden arches and an assortment of pizza temples, talk of fasting as a religious duty is almost ludicrous! If fasting exists at all in our time, it is in connection with dieting, and that is largely based on motivations that are either cosmetic or therapeutic. Few people recall that fasting in the Bible was a spiritual discipline that one undertook to get closer to God. The focus was not on the self, but on God, and I cannot help wondering if that little couplet that used to be quoted to those who quit smoking could well be recited for those who make such a show of their dieting: "Giving up eating too much isn't enough. It's giving up bragging about it that's tough."

But that is precisely what Isaiah's message to us is — a call to move beyond public displays of piety to a faith that touches every aspect of our private and public lives. It is no accident that behind the Greek word for piety is the Hebrew word for justice. What was a problem for the people of God in Isaiah's time is even a greater concern in our own age — namely, that the modern church is in danger of being swallowed up by our culture to the point where no one can even tell who are the followers of Jesus Christ. Let's listen again to the prophet's message about the built-in hazard in religion.

1. God's Approval Versus Human Applause

First, Isaiah calls us to remember that it is God's approval and not human applause that ultimately counts. Jesus echoed the same call when he urged his followers to go about prayer and almsgiving and self-denial as though we were enlisted in the divine Secret Service. Those acts are done for the eyes and ears of God, not for any approval from our fellow human beings. According to Jesus, those who pray on street corners and make a great public show of piety already have their reward: they receive the approval of others. But the reward they hoped for — to be found pleasing to God — this will be denied to them.

89

Now it is not easy to let one's piety be hidden. If one has a lovely voice and sings in the church choir, the temptation is almost irresistible to let one's voice sound out above the others. "Listen to me. Is not my voice beautiful? Am I not fortunate to have such a musical instrument?" What's more, it is so satisfying to let one's golden tones ring out above the ordinary noises made by fellow singers! To know that others are hearing the same lovely voice that rings in one's own ears; what could be sweeter? But is God glorified by such a display? No, says Isaiah! One does not need a public validation. If a tree falls in a forest and no one hears it, is there truly a sound? If one transposes that to the life of faithfulness, the answer is a solid yes. The hearing or seeing by others is not what makes our acts faithful. It is the faithfulness of God that is our validation.

How easily we forget that the emphasis in the Christian life is not on what we have done, but rather on what God has done for us in Christ. I read recently of how an outstanding Christian Sunday school teacher died and went to heaven. At the gate he was met by Saint Peter who began asking him some questions about his life on earth. Peter then explained that he would need a total of 100 points on this exam to enter heaven. "Well, I went to church almost every Sunday," said the man proudly. "That's good for one point," said Peter. "I taught Sunday school for 23 years," said the man, his confidence somewhat shaken. "Great," said Saint Peter, "that's worth another point."

The teacher was getting nervous, but he managed to say, "And I helped the elderly lady who was my neighbor as often as I could." "Fine," said Saint Peter. "That gives you three points. You have 97 left to go!" Speechless, the man fell to his knees, and cried, "All I've got left is the grace of my Savior, Jesus!" Gently Peter reached down and lifted the man to his feet, and said, "And that, sir, makes exactly 100! Welcome to heaven!" Isaiah of old reminds his people that it is God's approval, not human applause that counts in the kingdom of God.

2. Believing And Behaving

But Isaiah's message is also a call to God's people to close the gap between believing and behaving. What infuriated Isaiah was people who fasted on holy days, and then oppressed their workers the rest of the time. I think of the 18th century ship captain carrying slaves in the hold of his ship. The slaves were without sufficient food and water, and their situation was desperate. Yet the good captain decided to read his morning devotion on deck. He turned to the words in 1 John which say, "Beloved, let us love one another, for love is of God." From below decks came the cries of dying men, yet the captain did nothing. He told his crew, "It's not my problem. I am only a sailor."

Isaiah, in words that perhaps better describe our world than his own, appeals to people of faith "to loose the bonds of wickedness, to share your bread with the hungry, and to bring the homeless poor into your house." In those prophetic words, the prophet calls us to close the gap between our beliefs and our behavior. This is first a call for deeds of justice. Isaiah's words speak pointedly to those of us who live in a land of plenty in the midst of a world that is starving — a world where it is said that if every hungry person was lined up single file, the line would encircle the globe not once, not twice, but 25 times! Isaiah's call for deeds of justice along with pious behavior is echoed by Jesus in those famous words in Matthew 25. A modern writer has written:

> *I was hungry, and you formed a humanities club and discussed my hunger. Thank you.*
> *I was imprisoned, and you crept off quietly to your chapel and prayed for my release.*
> *I was naked, and in your mind, you debated the morality of my appearance.*
> *I was sick, and you knelt beside your bed and thanked God for your health.*
> *I was homeless, and you preached to me about the spiritual shelter of the love of God.*

91

I was lonely, and you left me alone to pray for myself.
You seem so holy, so close to God, but I am still hun-
gry, and lonely and cold.
What does it profit a person to page through their book
of prayers when the rest of the world is crying out for
help?[1]

Isaiah's message is also a plea to God's people to love and to show generosity in the same ways that God has loved us. Isaiah has no patience for those who claim that what happens in politics, in government, in society, in the business world, or in military affairs is of no concern to the church. For Isaiah, God is Lord over all of life, and that means that God is much more than a small compartment labeled "formal religion." God is holy, and a moral God demands moral holiness in all of life.

The familiar words of Sir George McCleod to the Iona Community in Scotland still speak of God's call to carry our faith into all of life. McCleod wrote: "I simply argue that the cross be raised again at the center of the marketplace as well as on the steeple of the church. I am for recovering the claim that Jesus was not crucified in a cathedral between two candles, but on a cross between two thieves, on the town garbage heap, at a place so cosmopolitan, they had to write his title in Hebrew, Latin and Greek; at the kind of place where cynics talk smut, soldiers gamble and thieves curse; because that is where Christ died, and that is what Christ died about, and that is where church people ought to be, and what church people should be about."

Closing the gap between belief and behavior is not something we will ever do in our human strength and wisdom, but in the power of God's Spirit, all things are possible. The answer to so much that is wrong in our world has come in Jesus Christ, who in reconciling us to God, brings us to a place where we can be reconciled to one another. Only then shall "light break forth like the dawn, and righteousness shall go before you."

Epiphany 6
Deuteronomy 30:15-20

The Illusion Of Neutrality

Charlie Moran, the old National League baseball umpire, always regarded himself and his decisions highly. He liked to make it clear to the ballplayers who was boss behind the plate. One day, in a very close play at home, the runner and the catcher eagerly awaited Charlie's decision. The umpire hesitated, and the catcher shouted, "Well, is he safe or is he out?" Moran pulled himself up to his full height, cleared his throat, and said to the catcher, "Mister, until I calls it, it ain't nothin' at all!"

Of all the illusions nursed by we modern people, none is more pathetic or dangerous than the illusion of neutrality. Neutrality is that notion that human beings can detach themselves from all crucial choices and decisions in life. Social neutrality straddles the fence of public opinion and refuses to come down on either side of the great social issues. Moral neutrality shows itself in broadminded tolerance which sees all matters of good and evil not in terms of black and white, but in terms of differing shades of grey. Spiritual neutrality chooses neither belief nor atheism, but leaves the matter of God's claim on our lives up in the air.

Picture, if you will, a person who tries to live under this dangerous illusion. Here is a person who works as a clerk in

93

a big store and lives quietly with his family in a modest suburban home. "I am a peaceful man," he is fond of saying. He has no enemies, simply because he has no strong convictions about anything. He rarely involves himself in an argument, and when discussions do arise at work or home, he never takes sides. Nobody knows where this man stands politically, how he votes, or whether he votes at all. In conversation with neighbors about the great problems of the day, he is much like the man who jumped on his horse and rode rapidly off in all directions! Even this man's children cannot draw their father into helping settle simple disputes or make basic life choices. He does attend church every week, but he leaves quickly so as not to offend his colleagues who have no use for the church. Once there was an issue that threatened to divide his congregation, but this fellow kept his feet firmly planted in both camps. The man is a moral acrobat! In all of life's major choices, he straddles the fence, believing in nothing, caring for nothing, loving nothing, and remaining alive, only because he has nothing worth dying for in his empty life.

Our modern society has made a kind of virtue out of openness and neutrality, but how sad it is to meet someone who lives with this form of self-deception. I once met a woman who told me that she would not become a Christian because there were too many obstacles in the path of belief. "I'm not an atheist, you understand, but I'm not convinced that God exists, or that Christianity is the right religion, so I am going to withhold judgment and consider the matter impartially." I only hope that woman gets off the fence pretty soon. You see, she is 87 years old, and her so-called neutrality is fast becoming academic!

In many ways, that's the same message from God that Moses was giving to the people of Israel as they stood on the threshold of the Promised Land. Moses says that to enter into a covenant with the Lord is to make a decision, to commit oneself wholly to God and God's way. This is one of the most explicit calls for decision that the Bible presents. Whether you are a Hebrew from long ago listening to Moses, or a modern person encountering these words in worship or study, you cannot put them aside. The most fundamental choice of life lies before those who have come to this boundary line. Indeed, the choice is life itself — or death; blessing — or curse.

Moses' call for decision about the great issue of life exposes three fundamental truths about the illusion of neutrality in our modern world.

1. A Luxury For Which Someone Must Pay

First, neutrality is a luxury for which somebody has to pay the price. Think for a moment of the thousands of Poles, French, Belgians and others who died from 1939-41 while we in America hid behind the charade of neutrality in the face of Hitler's Nazi War Machine that was bent on all out destruction. Those men and women in a real sense paid for our neutrality and lack of decisive action.

A little more than 100 years ago the slaves in our country were declared free. Their freedom came at terrific cost, not only because some Americans favored slavery, but also because a great majority of Americans held no strong convictions either way. People in high places tried to maintain a discreet posture of neutrality. What saved the Union was the unequivocal partisanship of Abraham Lincoln who struck out fearlessly on this crucial issue of human rights. Even as a young man, Lincoln had taken a stand in New Orleans where he saw slaves chained and whipped at the slave auction. Lincoln said to his friends, "By God, if I ever get a chance to hit this thing, I'll hit it hard." Speaking later in his presidential campaign, Lincoln told a crowd in New York, "There is no use groping about for some middle ground between right and wrong or in having a policy of 'don't care' on a question about which all true men do care."[1] Lincoln knew that neutrality is always a luxury for which someone has to pay. In fact, Lincoln is the one who paid with his own life, so that slavery might be eliminated from this nation.

The same truth is evident when we consider the church in today's society. A majority of people apparently are not opposed to the church and what it stands for. They are neither for the church or against it. They would describe themselves as neutral. Of course, if everyone assumed that posture, there would soon be no church to support or oppose. The church, as we know it, would pass out of existence, and with it would go the mainspring of Christianity — the one insitution that keeps alive the redemptive power of God's revelation in Christ. Some people can afford to be neither for or against the church, only because others continue to be stubbornly and devotedly for it. Thank God for the sometimes faithful few, who have been willing to pay the price to keep the doors of a church open. Neutrality is always a luxury for which someone must pay the price.

2. The Refusal To Choose Is A Choice

Consider also that Moses' challenging words expose another fallacy about the illusion of neutrality — the refusal to choose does itself consitute a choice. Jesus put the matter of choice very simply when he said, "The one who is not with me is against me." Moses reminds the Hebrews that the good life which is God's gift will not happen automatically. The life offered in the new land must be lived out by consciously choosing purity of life, justice and fairness, the honor of parents, respect of neighbors, and faithfulness to God. To live every other way said Moses is to choose the way of death and catastrophe.

Not to decide an issue is often to make a decision. I recall a time when I was growing up when the issue of Sunday closing became a referendum in our little town. It was a touchy issue. Many politicians spoke out of both sides of their mouths. Many pastors seemed to lose their voices. When the votes were counted, a handful of voters had decided to end Sunday closing in that town while the vast majority of people, unable to make up their minds, or unwilling to take a stand did not even vote "Yes" or "No." They found that their refusal to choose did itself constitute a choice.

We cannot avoid making a decision about the basic issues of life. The ultimate questions of life have to be answered one way or the other. For instance, does life make sense or is it simply nonsense? Is life a meaningless struggle, or is it nurtured in the purpose and goodness of Almighty God? Are the love, kindness and generosity we show in our finest moments indications of the true nature of life, or are they so much sentimental weakness? What is more important — people or things, individuals or institutions? Do governments exist to be served, or do they exist to serve? Is God real or not? Was Jesus a dreamer and a psychopathetic fool, or did he know how life at its best should be lived? Two choices — God's way or the God-denying way. Life forces them upon us. Whatever we believe with our minds, our lives are committed to one or the other. There can be no middle ground, no neutrality!

3. God Does Not Recognize Neutrals

From beginning to end, the message of the Bible is clear: God does not recognize neutrals. When it comes to the great moral and spiritual choices of life, God insists that we take a stand. In the dramatic scene in our scripture lesson for today, Moses stands before a people whose ancestors spent 400 years in slavery in Egypt until God led them out, divided the waters of the Red Sea, fed them manna from heaven, and gave them eternal laws to live by in a new land. In the light of all of God's dealings with them, the people must now decide once and for all whether to choose life or death, blessing or curse. From God's point of view, there is no neutrality.

No less dramatic is that scene at Shechem when Joshua again sets before the people the choice to serve the living God, or the pagan deities of Israel's new neighbors. "And if you be unwilling to serve the Lord, choose this day whom you will serve . . . but as for me and my house, we will serve the Lord (Joshua 24:14-15)." The same words are echoed by Elijah on Mount Carmel. Standing there before King Ahab and the 750

97

priests of Baal, and the uncommitted hosts of Israel, the crusty old prophet shouts, "How long will you go limping with two opinions? If the Lord is God, follow him, but if Baal, then follow him (1 Kings 18:21)."

If we ever had any doubts about how God feels about neutrality, the writer of the Book of Revelation dispels that doubt as he describes that large, successful, affluent congregation at Laodicea. From the description given, this is not a church at all, but a religious club to which the best people owe it to themselves to belong. On the great issues of the day, this congregation is neither cold nor hot, but sickeningly tepid. Therefore they made God sick! "So, because you are lukewarm," says the writer, "and neither cold nor hot, I will spew you out of my mouth (Revelation 3:16)."

One of Britain's great preachers, W. E. Sangster, went with his son to a cricket match between Surrey and Sussex. Before the start of the game, Dr. Sangster said to his little son, "Now, my boy, let's have none of your nonsense about 'May the best team win.' I don't want the best team to win. I want Surrey to win!" Much later, that young man in writing about his father, described him as "vehemently partisan not only towards sport, but more especially toward the great issues of life." Sangster saw all of life as a crucial conflict between the kingdom of Christ and the kingdom of Satan. He never nursed any illusions about being neutral. He wanted Jesus Christ to win.

No Christian can be neutral about Jesus Christ. We follow the most un-neutral person who ever lived. Jesus of Nazareth lived on this earth a life of perfect obedience to God, a life so completely committed to God's way, it inevitably brought him into conflict with those who opposed that way. It is the life God intends for us to live; and unless we are prepared to live it, and if need be to suffer for our commitment, then we identify ourselves not with Christ, but with those who nailed him to a cross. That is what Jesus meant when he punctured the illusion of neutrality by saying, "The one who is not for me is against me." Choose this day whom you will serve!

Epiphany 7
Isaiah 49:8-13

Is Anybody There?
Does Anybody Care?

In 1976 when our nation was celebrating its bicentennial, there was a delightful musical produced about those uneasy weeks in Philadelphia more than 200 years ago when our Declaration of Independence was being written and signed. Throughout the whole production of "1776," a courier from General Washington keeps breaking in on the proceedings of the Continental Congress with increasingly disheartening news from the New Jersey encampments. The seemingly endless debate drags on . . . 85 changes are made in the document . . . and 400 words are deleted. Suddenly the courier arrives with the terrible news that General Washington and his troops are in full retreat from New York. The General has but 5,000 volunteers while the British Regulars number more than 25,000 seasoned veterans. The production is so powerful that even sitting in the audience, you begin to feel the loneliness of Washington and his rag-tag army in the field, fighting for a cause in which no one seems to care. On goes the endless debate in Philadelphia while men are dying of exposure and disease.

Finally, the character who portrays John Adams, sings a song. It is a song that arises from the depths of his own heart, but it speaks for those in any age who question the ways of God as it asks, "Is Anybody There? Does Anybody Care?"

How often even those with the strongest of faith have uttered that same cry! Recall the prophet Elijah crying out in despair, "But now I only am left, for the children of Israel have forsaken their covenant, thrown down God's altars, and slain his prophets. O wretched man that I am!"

Jeremiah was a great believer in God, but in the midst of a bad time in his life, he felt God was nowhere to be found. "O God, art thou to me like a dried up brook when the waters fail?" Is anybody there? Does anybody care? Martin Luther, certainly no cynic, and surely a believer in God's mercy, nevertheless once cried out in rage, "My God, art thou dead?" Thomas Carlyle looked over the slums of London and groaned in disgust, "God sits in his heaven and does nothing." Is anybody there? Does anybody care?

Even the strongest people of faith wonder in those terrible moments when it seems as if God is silent, "Does this God really exist?" There is a story about a long-winded preacher, a short-winded preacher and the Easter Bunny who all entered a restaurant one evening and sat down together at a table. There was a $5 bill on the table, left as a tip for the waitress by the last customer. Suddenly all the lights went out. When the lights came back on, the $5 bill was missing. The question is which one of the three took the $5. The answer is the long-winded preacher, because everyone knows the other two don't really exist.

Is anybody there? Does anybody care? How often the Hebrew people had asked that same question during the nightmare of the Babylonian captivity. But now Babylon has fallen, and a return to their homeland is at least a possibility! But without the confident words of faith spoken by Isaiah in our reading for today, it is doubtful whether the downhearted exiles would ever have plucked up enough courage to return. Second Isaiah is addressing people who are so used to bondage, they lack the initiative to venture forth, now that the prison gates are thrown open. But in words that speak about God's providential care to despairing and questioning hearts in any age, Isaiah gives a triumphant "Yes" to the question, "Is there anybody there? Does anybody care?"

100

1. God Does Have A Plan

The prophet first reminds his people that the Living God has a plan for this world and that our lives are ruled, not by chance, or coincidence, or fate, but by the gracious providence of God. Wrote Isaiah, "Thus says the Lord, 'In a time of favor I have answered you, and in a day of salvation, I have helped you.' " God's apparent silence in our lives ought never to be mistaken for indifference.

Some years ago, Americans were humming a tune titled, "Que Sera, Sera" . . . Whatever will be, will be. It was a lovely song, but so far as the Word of God is concerned, it just is not true! Ours is not a God who, like some clockmaker, constructs some intricate mechanism, winds it up, sets it on the shelf, and then, just lets it tick, while God goes off to do something else. That is a situation where nobody's there and nobody cares.

Neither does the Bible picture a God who controls every detail of our lives, or one who puts a protective cocoon around us to keep us from bad things. That is a case where not only is somebody there, but that somebody "over cares" to the point where we would be little more than puppets on a string. Instead the Bible describes a Living God who has a plan for this world, and for our lives, but who works out that plan in such a marvelous way that our human freedom is preserved.

Back in the 1930s there was a Scottish golfer by the name of Bobby Cruikshank who played the game with glorious zest. During the Open of 1934, Bobby pitched to the green, and then watched anxiously as his ball fell short and landed in a brook. Suddenly, there was a shriek of joy from the assembled gallery. The ball had prankishly struck a rock in the brook, and bounced onto the green about a foot from the pin. The overjoyed Scot flung his club high in the air, doffed his cap to the crowd, and bowed low saying, "Thank you, God!" Suddenly the golf club came down and conked the zealous Scot right on the top of his head.

101

Now the Bible would say that God did not cause that golf ball to hit the rock, or the club to come down on the Scot's head. Those things are part of the good and the bad which God allows us as free children to experience in life. Nor does God cause cancer for some people, or earthquakes and plane crashes for others. Those are all realities of life in this risky world. Rather, the Word of God tells us, as Isaiah does, that God is a Shepherd leading the way for the sheep. God is a loving parent who shares our joys and heartaches in Jesus Christ, but does not manipulate or control all that happens to us.

Think about these matters on the human level. A little girl has a doll she loves. One day, however, the doll is broken, and the little girl weeps with a broken heart. At first as a parent, you want to run out and replace the broken doll with another, but somehow we know that life is not like that. The little girl must learn that some things break which can never be repaired or replaced. So as a loving parent, we hold her close, dry her tears, and assure her of our love and care.

Or, a little boy gets his first two-wheeler. But before long, he is on the ground with a scraped knee and a cut arm. Part of us wants to hold him close and never let him ride again, so he will never get hurt. But life is not like that, and if he would ever know the joy of riding a bike, then he must learn to live with bumps and bruises and we must let him go.

Those are very human pictures, but that is exactly how the Bible describes a God who has a plan to work out in this world. Like a wise and loving parent, God shares our falling and rising, our weeping and our laughter, and somehow God weaves it all into a grand design.

2. God Is At Work In Everything

Isaiah continues his encouragement to his people by insisting that God is at work for good in everything that happens to them. Picturing God as a shepherd, the prophet says, "They shall feed along the ways, on all bare heights shall be their pasture; they shall not hunger or thirst, neither scorching wind or sun shall smite them, for he who has pity on them will lead them by springs of water.'' God not only has a plan for his people, but as they go forth, they know that in everything that happens to them, good or bad, God is at work. I recall a man who once said to me in a moment of great despair, ''God moves in a mischievous way, his blunders to perform.'' But that is not the God Isaiah describes, or the God whom we know in Jesus Christ! We may not understand why sickness comes, or accidents happen, or why we sometimes fail in spite of our best efforts. But the Bible is unanimous in its conviction that God is at work for good in everything that happens to us.

The apostle Paul certainly came to believe this after many long dark nights for his soul when he questioned God's ways. Writing from a Roman prison cell, Paul finally was able to catch a glimpse of God at work in his imprisonment, giving him the opportunity to write letters of faith that still change human hearts today. Another great missionary of the church, David Livingstone, had his heart set on going to China for the Lord. But his way was blocked. Yet, trusting that God was at work even in his disappointment, Livingstone went to Africa, the last place on earth he ever dreamed of living. But it was David Livingstone's ministry that first introduced Africans to the love of Jesus Christ, and today, Africa is the fastest growing Christian continent in the world. In everything, God is at work for good!

3. God Is The Sole And Sufficient Resource

Isaiah concludes this stirring message with the reminder that God is the sole and sufficient resource that his people need as they venture forth back to their homeland. The prophet says, ''For the Lord has comforted his people and will have compassion on his afflicted.'' Those words were echoed many years later by William Bradford as he recorded the struggle of the Pilgrims at Plymouth Colony. ''They had no friends to welcome them, nor inns to entertain or refresh their weather-beaten bodies, no houses or much less towns to repair to, to seek for succor. What could now sustain them but the Spirit of God and his grace (History of Plymouth Plantation)?''

Sometimes it is only in our brokenness and utter desolation that we remember that God is our sole and sufficient resource. That great missionary David Livingstone, may have been God's vehicle for opening up the continent of Africa to the Christian gospel, but never forget that his success story began back in Scotland where a humble pastor was so discouraged, he was tempted to give up the ministry altogether. In one whole year's work in his parish, this poor pastor had brought only one person to a saving knowledge of Jesus Christ, and that person was a mere boy. What possible good could a young boy make in the kingdom of God? The pastor judged his life a failure, but the God who is our sole and sufficient resource used that pastor's ministry to touch the heart of the young David Livingstone, who in turn, touched the lives of thousands for Jesus Christ! As Paul so aptly wrote to the Corinthian church, ''We have this treasure in earthen vessels to show that the transcendent power belongs to God.''

Is anybody there? Does anybody care? Isaiah and the other writers of the Bible answer that question with a triumphant ''Yes!'' There may be many times in our human experience where we question where God is in all that happens to us. But this much is certain: We can always rejoice, because in the end, our God will be triumphant.

When actress Deborah Kerr was involved in the making of the epic motion picture, *Quo Vadis*, an interviewer reminded her that at one point in the film, she is tied to a stake in the Roman Coliseum with savage lions rushing at her. The interviewer asked, ''Weren't you afraid at that moment?'' The actress laughingly replied, ''Not at all! You see, I had read the script to the end, and I knew that Robert Taylor would rush in to rescue me!''

In the resurrection of Jesus Christ, we have been privileged to read the script of God's plan on this earth, and we know that it ends with the triumphant promise of our Risen Lord: ''Be of good cheer, for I have overcome the world!''

Epiphany 8
Leviticus 19:1-2, 9-18

The Recovery Of Reverence

Once upon a time there was a college professor named A Squared. A Squared lived in Flat Land. Everything in Flat Land had just two dimensions: height and breadth. Nothing in Flat Land had any depth! The people lived in flat houses, ate flat meals, drank flat colas, thought flat thoughts and lived flat lives. Everything was flat. If a person turned sideways, you could not even see that individual!

A Squared taught mathematics at the local university. One night he threw a party for some of his colleagues on the faculty. Upstairs his precocious little son, Pentagon, tried to sleep. As the little boy tossed fitfully, he began to dream. In his dream Pentagon imagined that he was suddenly in a world where everything had not only height and breadth, but depth as well. What a difference that made! Houses and trees and especially girls looked so different! Pentagon felt different. Life had a whole new dimension and it was wonderful.

But then his dream ended and the boy awoke. However, Pentagon could not keep a dream like that to himself. Jumping out of bed, he ran downstairs in his bare feet and rumpled pajamas to tell the guests at his father's party that there was a whole new dimension to life. People did not have to go on living flat little lives anymore, thinking only flat little thoughts. There was a whole new dimension to life — the dimension of depth. A Squared was flabergasted! Not only was he embarrassed over his little son's behavior, but he could not keep the boy quiet! The party ended in a shambles.

The next day little Pentagon talked about his dream to anyone who would listen. He kept stamping his foot and insisting that there was another dimension to life. But the people of Flat Land thought the poor boy was sick, and they took him off to a mental hospital. But his father, A Squared, did not sleep well that night. He kept thinking to himself: Maybe my little son is right, maybe there is more to life, maybe things could be different!

That is only a make-believe story, of course, but I wonder if there are not many people who would describe their everyday lives like that of the citizens of Flat Land. For them, there is little awareness of the past or the future. There is only the present as if the world began last Saturday night. Life seems to be lived in just one plane — the human. There is no awareness of anything beyond us, or anything above us, or anything bigger than ourselves.

In many ways our contemporary society has lost the dimension of the holy and the sacred. Our lives lack depth, because we have smashed everything sacred in sight. Our society smashes sacred days like the Sabbath. As the very foundation of a stable social structure, and as a safeguard of personal freedom, God gave the human race some common sense rules, one of which said, "Remember the sabbath day to keep it holy." Holiness denotes difference, the principle being that we make one day in seven different from other days. This, according to God's plan, was a day set aside to acknowledge and honor and worship God. But today our secular society tramples over the sabbath as vandals trample over a flower garden. The same thing has happened to sacred festivals like Christmas. In our secular society we dare to use God's Son to increase our financial profits and to enhance our sentimental pleasure.

Our society smashes not only sacred days, but the most sacred relationships where God has always been present. People today request that God's name not be mentioned in their wedding service. Yet, in almost every Christian tradition, there are the solemn words, "God established marriage . . ." The very institution of marriage, a man and woman committing themselves unconditionally to a life together, is a gift from God and therefore sacred.

Moreover, our contemporary society smashes the values that were sacred to past generations. When nothing is held sacred, the sense of moral judgment and spiritual muscle withers away. A person's body is no longer sacred. The crime of rape is more prevalent in the United States today than anywhere in the civilized world. Property is no longer sacred. People steal everything from hotel towels to the files of psychiatrists and see nothing wrong in these actions. Employees last year stole a record $10 billion in goods from their employers! No longer does the Golden Rule apply in everyday life. Today it has become a case of "Do unto others as you would have them do unto you, only do it first!" We have become a generation that has lost the dimension of holy. Running through our art, our novels, our movies, our television and all of life, is a fundamental irreverence toward the God revealed in Jesus Christ.

Our situation is not unlike the hapless parents of a boy named Bobby whose bad behavior exceeded everyone's expectations. It was the boy's birthday and the father suggested to the mother that they give him a bicycle for his birthday. "Do you suppose the bike will help improve his bad behavior?" asked his mother. "No," said the desperate father, "But it will spread his bad behavior over a wider area!"

But the ancient Book of Leviticus speaks to our times in a rich and relevant way. Many people think of this book as nothing more than a dusty old record of rules pertaining to early Hebrew life. But in the words of today's reading, there are two fundamental truths that can help us recover the dimension of reverence missing in so much of modern life.

1. Recover Our Need For God

These words are first and foremost a call to recover our need for the Living God. God's word through Moses to the people is, "You shall be holy, for I the Lord your God am holy." Holiness on our part demands an attitude of reverence. The source of trouble in our irreverent society is our delusion that we have outgrown our need for the Living God.

A few years ago a pastor friend of mine accompanied a group of pilgrims on a visit to Israel and the Holy Land. The group stopped at a kibbutz on the eastern shore of the Sea of Galilee. Their guide was a man named Moses Ezekiel, who pointed with pride to the miracles that had been accomplished by the Israeli people since taking possession of this land in 1948. Here were rows of tidy houses, and vineyards that yielded an abundant harvest. Here were date palms from which one could pluck the succulent fruit. There were barns filled with pure-bred cattle, and an auditorium for symphony concerts and lectures. But amidst all these signs of a thriving civilization, there was one notable exception. There was no house of worship — a rather startling omission for a people who have bequeathed such a rich heritage to the world.

My friend asked why there was no synagogue, and Moses Ezekiel began to laugh. Finally he said, "Why build a synagogue when no one wants to pray? Is it not better to spend the money on something useful like a tractor?" My pastor friend was amazed at the answer. He could only think of another man named Moses who warned the Hebrew people some 3,000 years ago not to forget the Living God when they came into the land of promise. Said Moses, "Beware lest you say in your heart that my power and the might of my hand has gotten me this wealth . . . If you forget the Lord your God, I solemnly warn you this day that you shall surely perish from the earth (Deuteronomy 8)."

The writer of Leviticus speaks the same message to us in the midst of our prosperity and plenty: "I am the Lord your God." The lesson of history from ancient Egypt to Nazi

Germany is that any nation which does not have reverence for a power higher and greater than itself will perish from the earth. We ignore God's claim on our lives at our own peril.

There was once a famous Roman general who won a great victory. A triumphal celebration was held upon his return to Rome. His legions marched before him and then came all his captives in their chains and wagons filled with the spoils of war. Finally came the general in his chariot. The crowds were cheering wildly as he passed by and it was a proud and wonderful moment for the victorious soldier. But a slave riding with the general in his chariot leaned over and said to the great leader, "General, remember you are only a man!" That is the relevant message from the writer of Leviticus to our generation — a fervent call to remember our need for God, and the claim of God on all human life.

2. Reverence Brings Respect

The second fundamental truth in these ancient words for our time is the reminder that without reverence for God, there will be no respect for persons, for property or for justice. Clearly, the author of this ancient book had the Ten Commandments in mind as the grand design for human life intended by our Creator. Today, lots of people question the value of these ancient commandments. In fact in the city of Pittsburgh, a copy of the Ten Commandments is engraved on a wall in the city zoo where many rare birds are housed. This has caused more than a few people to comment that the Ten Commandments in our time are strictly for the birds!

But reverence for God is what makes possible our human respect for parents, for human life, for marriage, for property and for justice. The famous Quaker writer, Elton Trueblood, once called the Ten Commandments, God's Charter of Respect." Trueblood insists that too often, we have seen the commandments in their negative form. Positively written, the commandments become God's guideline for how a society can

109

live in mutual respect:

Above all else love God alone:
Bow down to neither wood nor stone.
God's name refuse to take in vain:
The sabbath rest with care maintain.
Respect your parents all your days:
Hold sacred human life always.
Be loyal to your chosen mate:
Steal nothing, neither small nor great.
Report with truth your neighbor's deed:
And rid your mind of selfish greed.[1]

That is the Bible's message about respect, but the words would have no meaning without Leviticus' reminder that, "I am the Lord your God!" That is almost the same reminder that precedes the commandments in the Bible: "I am the Lord your God who brought you out of the land of Egypt, out of the house of bondage. Therefore . . ." That is the basis for all reverence — God's everlasting claim upon our lives. Without that sacred sense that all of life belongs to God, there will be no respect for persons, for property, or for justice in our society.

So let this ancient word from Leviticus call us to a new sense of reverence for God and respect for one another. "And the Lord said to Moses, 'Say to all the congregation of people of Israel, you shall be holy; for I the Lord your God am holy.'"

Transfiguration
Exodus 24:12-18

Lessons From The Mountaintop

Frederick Buechner in his book, *Peculiar Treasures*, writes about Moses in the following way: "Whenever Hollywood cranks out a movie about Moses, they always give the part to somebody like Charlton Heston with some fake whiskers glued on. The truth of it is, he probably looked a lot more like Tevye the milkman after 10 rounds with Mohammed Ali. Moses up there on the mountain with his sore feet and aching back serves as a good example of the fact that when God puts the finger on people, their troubles have just begun! Hunkered down in the cleft of a rock, Moses had been allowed to see the Glory itself passing by, and although all God let him see was the back part, it was something to hold on to for the rest of his life."[1]

Mountaintop experiences in our faith journey become those moments of revelation that give us something to hold on to for the rest of our lives. That certainly is the kind of experience Moses had on Mount Sinai, and the kind of experience our Lord had with Peter, James and John on the Mount of Transfiguration. Any experience in which we recognize the Living God can be a transfiguration. It may take place on the summit of a mountain, or as we kneel in prayer on a wooden floor at sea level. It can happen in the midst of a service of worship

111

where God becomes dramatically real to us, and we know beyond a shadow of a doubt that Christ is our Living Lord and Savior. So as we celebrate the Transfiguration of our Lord, let us consider some spiritual lessons from the mountaintop.

1. The Value Of Spiritual Mountaintops

Let us consider first the lasting value of mountaintop revelations. To the ancient Hebrew mind, there was something mystical about mountaintops. Such places were associated with God's dwelling place. The cosmology of the Bible was that of ancient times, which saw the earth as a flat plain floating on a bed of water and protected from more water overhead by a dome-shaped firmament, or sky. Beyond the firmament and the water it held back was heaven and the throne of God. With that ancient three-storied view of the universe, it was only natural that mountaintops would achieve mystical significance. For both Moses receiving the Ten Commandments atop Mount Sinai and Jesus receiving the blessing of God on the Mount of Transfiguration, the experience was one that shaped not only their own future, but that of the people of God for many years to come.

Mountaintop experiences have that kind of lasting effect on those who experience them. There was once a father and son who had achieved a really good relationship with each other. Among their many good times together, one experience stood out above all others. It was a hike up a particular mountain where they seemed to reach the height of a beautiful friendship. After they returned home, there inevitably came a day when things did not seem to run as smoothly. The father rebuked the son and the son spoke sharply in return. An hour later the air between father and son had cleared. "Dad," said the boy, "whenever it starts to get like that again, let's one of us remind each other of that wonderful day we had on the mountain."

So it was agreed. In a few weeks, another misunderstanding occurred. The boy was sent to his room in tears. After a
while, the father decided to go up and see the boy. He was
still angry until he saw a piece of paper pinned to the door.
The boy had penciled two words in large letters, "The Mountain." That symbol was powerful enough to restore the relationship between father and son. That is the nature of
mountaintop experiences — they have a lasting value which
shapes our spiritual lives for years to come. The law which
Moses received atop Mount Sinai, and the salvation which
Jesus made possible on Mount Calvary are but two examples
of how important spiritual mountaintops are in our faith
journey.

2. The Mystery In Mountaintop Experience

A second lesson that comes out of Moses' experience on
the mountaintop is the element of mystery which always ac-
companies such revelations. Our modern world is often intoler-
ant of mystery. Ours is an age which is obsessed with the idea
of knowing and explaining everything. A story is told of a little boy whose father expressed the usual before dinner command: "Hurry up and wash your hands and come to prayers."
As the boy went toward the bathroom, he was heard to mut-
ter, "Germs and Jesus, germs and Jesus! That's all I hear
around here, and I can't see either one of them!"
But the Living God always comes to us in surprising and
mysterious ways. The revelation we receive is not always im-
mediately clear and unambiguous. If it were, there would be
no need for faith. Moses on the mountain alone with God reminds us that we will never fully understand the ways God
breaks into our lives, nor can we judge others' mountaintop
experiences by our own. For some, God may become more
real in a magnificent manifestation on a mountaintop, while
for others, it is that still small voice within that brings us into
the presence of the Living God.

In almost all occasions in the Bible where people experience God, there is mention of a cloud. In Jewish thought, the cloud or "Shekinah" was the age old symbol of the Divine Presence. Moses sees God in the cloud. It was a cloud that led the people of God through the wilderness. It was a cloud that filled the Temple after Solomon built it. At the Ascension, Jesus is received up into a cloud which signified that he has been taken up into the nearer presence of God. On the Mount of Transfiguration, Peter experiences an overwhelming sense of what theologians call the mysterium tremendum. It was that mysterious and yet wondrous experience in the clouds that resolved Peter's doubts forever.

3. The Temptation Of The Mountaintop

In almost all accounts of mountaintop experiences in the Bible, those who have the experience face the temptation of wanting to cling to the moment forever. It is a tragedy when people stop and build upon one period in their religious thinking. There are those whose understanding of God has never progressed beyond the "now I lay me down to sleep" stage. Conversely, there are those who have rejected religion in their early years because of some unfortunate experience with a pastor, priest or Sunday school teacher. They put the freeze on their own personal spiritual history at the moment. Their minds are closed to the possibility of an adult faith.

I am sure you have seen the ads on television: a group of friends sitting around a campfire. A clean, clear mountain stream rushing by. A skillet filled with fish. A tub filled with "Old Milwaukee." And one of the friends says to the others, "Fellows, it doesn't get any better than this!" We have all had those kinds of experiences. Everything is just right. It cannot get any better. We want to hang on to the moment and stay on the mountaintop forever. The problem is that the God we discover on the mountaintop is a God who is always on the move. Our God is never stationed in one place. The biblical

114

God is like a Methodist preacher: an itinerant who doesn't stay in one place forever!

Moments of high religious ecstasy are important, just as moments of intense emotion are important in a marriage, but you cannot build a marriage upon those moments alone. Nor can we build all of our faith on the memory of a great moment with God. God calls us forward into the future, and that usually means down from the mountain to meet the problems of the marketplace. Ernest Hemingway once wrote a book about his early days as a writer in Paris. He titled the book, *A Moveable Feast*. In 1950 he wrote, "If you are lucky enough to have lived in Paris as a young man, then wherever you go for the rest of your life, it stays with you, for Paris is a moveable feast." I do not know about Paris, but the presence of God is a moveable feast. Even when we leave the mountaintop, we do not leave God behind. In fact, it is God who leads the way!

4. The Urgency Of Spiritual Mountaintops

Still a fourth lesson we can discern in Moses' experiences on Mount Sinai is the urgency with which he is compelled by God to head back down the mountain with a stone tablet under each arm. Every genuine encounter with the Living God turns out to be an urgent call to discipleship at the foot of the mountain. God does not give us spiritual trips away from the real world; God has a tendency to thrust us back into the thick of it! There are needs to be met at the foot of the mountain. There is a world desperately in need of a vision of God, or the touch of someone who has had a vision of God, and who wants to share it. Real Christianity is not just what happens in the sanctuary; it is ultimately what we do in the real world which counts.

A few years ago a new pastor was called to a neighboring church in our community. The local newspaper was supposed to announce "The Installation of Dr. Jones as Pastor of

First Baptist Church." But instead, the paper printed in bold headline, "The Insulation of Dr. Jones as Pastor of First Baptist Church." Many Christians would prefer insulation to installation when it comes to doing the real work of the kingdom! Sometimes living as a Christian amidst the squabbles, the complaints, the pettiness, and the pain of life in the real world is less than glamorous. Nevertheless, God calls us to share our faith and our experience of God outside the safety of the church in a world that God still loves, and wants to redeem in the name of our Lord Jesus Christ.

When Dr. Elizabeth Kubler-Ross was doing research for her famous book on death and dying, she met a woman who was a member of the cleaning staff in a large hospital. This woman spent her days cleaning floors, emptying wastebaskets and tidying up patients' rooms. The hospital staff, however, began to notice that each time this woman finished cleaning the room of a dying patient, that person was invariably more content and more at peace. The woman explained to Dr. Kubler-Ross that she had known a lot of fear and tragedy in her life, as well as good times when others helped her know of God's love. She had been up and she had been down the mountain. The worst time was when her three-year-old son was ill with pneumonia. She brought him to the public health clinic, and he died in her arms while she waited her turn. All of this could have embittered her, but she said to Kubler-Ross, "You see, doctor, the dying patients are just like old acquaintances to me, and I'm not afraid to touch them, to talk to them, or to offer them hope." The hospital decided to promote this woman to "Special Counselor To The Dying."

And is that not the call of God to each one of us — to be Special Counselors To The Dying? We cannot stay on the mountaintop forever. There are so many lives to be touched with the love of Christ down there in the valley where we live. This is the most important lesson from the mountaintop. Let us go forth to touch others as God has touched us.

Notes

"Something's Coming"

1. "Something's Comin' " from *West Side Story*. Music by Leonard Bernstein; Lyrics by Stephen Sondheim. Copyright 1957 © (Renewed) by Leonard Bernstein and Stephen Sondhaim. Jalni Publications, Inc., U.S. and Canadian Publisher. G. Schirmer, Inc., worldwide print rights and publisher for the rest of the world. International Copyright Secured. All Rights Reserved. Used by permission.

Christmas Preparations We Often Forget

1. A. Leonard Griffith, *God's Time And Ours,* Abingdon Press, Nashville, Tennessee, 1964. Used by permission.

2. *The Guideposts Christmas Treasury,* page 234, Guideposts Associates, Carmel, New York, 1972. Used by permission.

The Baby Who Changes Everything

1. *The Guideposts Christmas Treasury,* page 291, Guideposts Associates, Carmel, New York, 1972. Used by permission.

What Is God Like?

1. *The Guideposts Christmas Treasury,* page 125, Guideposts Associates, Carmel, New York, 1972. Used by permission.

2. *The Touch Of The Master's Hand,* by Myra Brooks Welch, copyrighted 1957 by the Brethren Press. Used by permission.

"So, What's New?"

1. "When The Cheering Stops," a sermon by Hugh Litchfield, printed in the *Master Sermon Series,* 1991, pages 61-62, published by Cathedral Directories, Madison Heights, Michigan. Used by permission.

Mission Possible
1. "Take The Time," by Miriam Therese Winter, published in *Women Prayer, Women Song, Resources For Ritual,* page 244, Meyer Stone, Oak Park, Illinois, 1987. Used by permission.

Improving Your Serve
1. Charles Swindoll, *Improving Your Serve,* page 19, Word Books, Waco, Texas, 1981. Used by permission.

Rejoice In The Lord
1. Quoted in sermon by the Rev. Robert Holland, September 26, 1971, Presbyterian Church On The Green, Morristown, New Jersey.

The Bottom Line
1. J. Elliott Corbett, *The Prophets On Main Street,* page 23, John Knox Press, Atlanta, Georgia, 1978. Used by permission.

2. Martin Luther King Jr., *Strength To Live,* pages 6-7, Fortress Press, Philadelphia, Pennsylvania. Used by permission.

Religion's Built-in Hazard
1. Quoted in OAKLEAVES, the Newsletter of the Basking Ridge Presbyterian Church, Basking Ridge, New Jersey, March, 1981.

The Illusion Of Neutrality
1. A. Leonard Griffith, *Illusion Of Our Culture,* page 35, Word Books, Waco, Texas, 1969. Used by permission.

The Recovery Of Reverence
1. Elton Trueblood, *The Company Of The Committed,* page 97, Harper Brothers, New York, 1961. Used by permission.

Lessons From The Mountaintop
1. Frederick Buechner, *Peculiar Treasures,* page 110, Harper and Row, New York, New York, 1979. Used by permission.

www.ingramcontent.com/pod-product-compliance
Lightning Source LLC
LaVergne TN
LVHW051649080426

835511LV00016B/2575